Careers in
Environmental
Conservation

Careers in Environmental Conservation

Fifth Edition

VIVIEN DONALD

KOGAN PAGE
CAREERS SERIES

First published in 1982
Second edition 1986
Third edition 1988
Fourth edition 1989
All entitled Careers in Conservation by John McCormick
Fifth edition 1992, reprinted with revisions 1993

Apart from any fair dealing for the purposes of research or private study, or criticism or review, as permitted under the Copyright, Designs and Patents Act, 1988, this publication may only be reproduced, stored or transmitted, in any form or by any means, with the prior permission in writing of the publishers, or in the case of reprographic reproduction in accordance with the terms of licences issued by the Copyright Licensing Agency. Enquiries concerning reproduction outside those terms should be sent to the publishers at the undermentioned address:

Kogan Page Limited
120 Pentonville Road
London N1 9JN

© Kogan Page Limited 1982, 1986, 1988, 1989, 1992

British Library Cataloguing in Publication Data

A CIP record for this book is available from the British Library.

ISBN 0-7494-0523-6

Typeset by DP Photosetting, Aylesbury, Bucks
Printed and bound in Great Britain by
Biddles Limited, Guildford and Kings Lynn

Contents

Part 1

1. **What is Environmental Conservation?**   9
   The Voluntary Sector 11; The Professional Sector 11; The Government Sector and Statutory Bodies 12

2. **Conservation Issues**   13
   Species Conservation 13; Population 14; Third World Development 14; Energy 14; Land Use Planning 15; The Oceans 15; Pollution 15; Forestry 16; Desertification 16; Waste 16; Education 17

3. **Careers in the Voluntary Sector**   18
   Introduction 18; Openings and Opportunities 19; The World Wide Fund for Nature 21; Friends of the Earth 22; The Centre for Alternative Technology 23; Greenpeace 24; Marine Conservation Society 24; Whale and Dolphin Conservation Society 25; British Trust for Conservation Volunteers 25; The Wildlife Trusts Partnership 25

4. **Resource Management**   28
   Introduction 28; Town and Country Planning 28; Forestry 30; The Water Industry 32; The Energy Industry 32; Landscape Architecture 33; Surveying 35; Park and Recreation Management 36; Working in Industry 38; Working in Agriculture 39

5. **Working for the Government**   41
   Introduction 41; Openings for School Leavers 41; Openings for Graduates 42; Relevant Government Departments 42

6. **Working for Statutory Bodies**   51
   Introduction 51; English Nature 51; Scottish Natural Heritage 53; Countryside Council for Wales 54; The Countryside Commission 54; The National Parks 55

7. **Education and Research**   59
   Introduction 59; Environmental Education 59; Research Opportunities 63

6   Careers in Environmental Conservation

8. **Opportunities for Scientists** 65
Introduction 65; Biology 65; Botany 66; Zoology 66; Ecology 66; Marine and Freshwater Biology 66; Oceanography 67; Biochemistry 67; Soil Science 67; Maths and Chemistry 67; Other Sciences 67

9. **Film-making, Photography and Writing** 71
Introduction 71; Film-making 71; Photography 73; Writing 74

10. **Working Overseas** 76
Introduction 76; Working with a British Organisation 76; Working with an International Organisation 77; Working with a Voluntary Aid Agency 77; Undertaking Research Projects 78; Emigrating or Settling Abroad 78

11. **Finding and Applying for Jobs** 80
Introduction 80; Know the Field 80; Know Your Interests 80; Make Yourself Valuable 81; Know Where to Find the Jobs 81; Be Prepared and Persistent 81; Future Prospects 82

Part 2

12. **University and College Courses and Qualifications** 85
Countryside Conservation and Management 85; Other Environmental and Management Courses 87; Science and Applied Science 89; Forestry 92; Landscape Architecture 92; Town and Country Planning 93

13. **Useful Journals** 95

14. **Useful Addresses** 99
Voluntary Bodies 99; Resource Management 101; Government Bodies 102; Statutory Bodies 103; Education and Research 103; Science Bodies 104; International Interest 104

Part 1

Chapter 1

What is Environmental Conservation?

Conservation means saving something for later use. 'Saving' can mean protecting, husbanding, managing or maintaining, and 'later use' can mean study, enjoyment or careful consumption. The principal concern of conservation is *using* nature and natural resources rationally and intelligently, thereby avoiding waste and ecological degradation.

Natural resources include everything from the food that we eat and the water we drink to the energy, air, soil, forests, lakes, rivers, wetlands and oceans that support our way of life. Most of these resources are renewable, ie they replace themselves. Managed carefully, they will supply our needs indefinitely. But mismanagement, waste and careless destruction has meant that many resources, such as fossil fuels, arable land and fisheries, are diminishing rapidly and the quality of our environment is suffering as a result.

All life on earth is confined to the biosphere, the thin skin on the surface of the planet that comprises the oceans, the atmosphere and the earth's land surface. Within the biosphere lives a complex community of several million different animal and plant species, all dependent upon one another for the basic essentials of life – air, water, food, warmth and shelter. Under natural circumstances this community is self-supporting, and renews itself, but the dominance of human beings has shifted this balance.

In their most primitive state, humans lived a hunter-gatherer life-style that was not far removed from that of other primates. But as they evolved greater intelligence, the demands they made on their environment grew. They developed a complex social structure, cultural values, and an intellect that needed stimulation. Buildings and towns replaced trees and caves as homes; diet became more complex; clothes, cosmetics and jewellery replaced animal skins; and agriculture and trades developed to accommodate and supply the new level of demand. As a result human activity had ever more visible effects on the environment. Forests were cleared for farms, roads and towns; metals and minerals were mined; rivers were dammed and diverted; plants were exploited for food and drugs; and animals were hunted and domesticated.

Until about 200 years ago the environmental impact of these activities was limited; however, the Industrial Revolution changed the effects considerably. Increasingly efficient industrial techniques created an even heavier demand on natural resources. Agriculture both expanded and intensified. Trading networks emerged needing roads, railways, canals and ports. Energy needs multiplied and fossil fuels were exploited intensively – first coal and then gas and oil. Progress in medical care cut down mortality rates and lengthened life expectancy, so that the world's population doubled between 1800 and 1900. More people meant a greater demand for food, water, energy, land and shelter.

In North America, concern at the uncontrolled slaughter of animals like the buffalo, at the destruction of forests and plant life, and at the inroads being made into the wilderness by the westward spread of settlement, led naturalists to campaign for the protection of areas of particular natural beauty. Consequently, the first national parks were created at Yellowstone and Yosemite at the end of the nineteenth century.

As more problems and threats were identified, conservation groups were set up and more people became professional conservationists. In Britain, the creation of the Royal Society for the Protection of Birds, the National Trust, and the Fauna and Flora Preservation Society followed in quick succession.

However, it was only after the Second World War, when people really began to understand that destruction of the environment was a global problem, that conservation began to establish itself. The first international organisation devoted to nature protection was the International Union for Conservation of Nature and Natural Resources (IUCN), founded in 1948.

Efforts to conserve wildlife and set up protected reserves and national parks grew during the 1950s and early 1960s, but it soon became obvious that threats to wildlife and nature were only one symptom of many far more deep-rooted problems. The dangers of pollution were widely recognised for the first time in the 1960s and rapid population growth caused much alarm. The ecological implications of agricultural and other forms of development were studied in detail, highlighting the crucial need to plan and carefully manage natural resources.

During the period of protest in the 1960s and early 1970s, the environment became a popular public issue and a wider understanding of the subject emerged. In 1972, the United Nations Conference on the Human Environment, held in Stockholm, helped people to realise that the problems of the natural environment were not separate from human society and that human beings were totally dependent on the well-being of the biosphere. The unregulated clearing of forests was linked to soil erosion and flooding; human pressure on marginal land on the edge of deserts was blamed for increasing the spread of desert conditions; and rising oil prices helped to focus the public's attention on the limits to the world's oil supply and the need for alternative sources of energy. It became clear that the welfare of the natural environment had far-reaching social, economic and political implications.

In the last 30 years there has been a sudden and marked growth in our desire to find out more about the natural environment. Scientific research and discovery are continually teaching us more about the capacity of the earth to support life. The environment has become a political issue, spawning Green parties in some countries and government ministries in others.

Not surprisingly, there has been a rapid growth in the number of people working in environmental conservation. At present, almost all openings are in one of three sectors – the voluntary, professional, or government sectors.

The Voluntary Sector

Although conservation and environmental management is gradually becoming a part of government policy, most of the work in Britain is still carried out by voluntary and other non-governmental organisations. Charities still provide much of the money, campaign groups much of the publicity and pressure for change, private research bodies much of the basic data and information, and volunteers many of the human resources.

Most of these groups have well-established contacts with local and national government, and are working towards making conservation part of the law and encouraging government interest. At the same time, they are trying to mobilise public opinion to strengthen their case. The character of voluntary bodies has altered in recent years to cope with changing needs. Where they used to be founded and funded by enthusiasts, they are quickly becoming more professional and more politically active (although they will take care not to compromise their charitable status).

Where voluntary bodies used to employ almost anyone who was committed to the cause and was willing to work hard for little pay, they are now more selective – enthusiasm and commitment alone are no longer enough. Employers now look for sound qualifications, abilities and experience that can be put to active and effective use. To attract more professional people, many of the larger charities are now paying more professional salaries.

Job opportunities in the voluntary field are described in more detail in Chapter 3.

The Professional Sector

Not all professional planners would think of themselves as conservationists; indeed, they are often criticised for their lack of environmental concern. Yet how well or how badly the environment is managed ultimately comes down to the attitudes of the new professionals – town and country planners, foresters, energy consultants, agriculturalists, surveyors, landscape architects, and water, soil, and land use planners.

Many professional planners are directly responsible for implementing government policy; others work for public or private companies. All make decisions that affect environmental quality in one way or another, and generally become involved in the trend towards more carefully considered environmental management, based on a greater understanding of the structure and limits of natural resources.

For those with an interest in environmental management, resource planning is an effective (if sometimes frustratingly bureaucratic) outlet for their energies. By their very nature, however, careers in this field demand a high degree of training and relevant experience.

Job opportunities in resource management are described in more detail in Chapter 4.

The Government Sector and Statutory Bodies

This sector has enjoyed particular growth in recent years as governments have given more thought to the natural environment. The Department of the Environment, which was created in 1970, has led to new job opportunities for conservationists, even though the natural environment is only a small part of its work.

Other relevant government departments include the Department of Energy, the Overseas Development Administration, the Natural Environment Research Council, the Ministry of Agriculture, Fisheries and Food and the Forestry Commission.

The last 30 years have seen the establishment of new statutory conservation bodies. These are usually active in managing national parks, nature reserves and other protected areas, and in undertaking environmental research. In the UK these responsibilities are shared between a coalition of organisations, including English Nature, the Countryside Council for Wales, the Scottish Natural Heritage Agency, the Countryside Commission, and a network of national park authorities, the National Rivers Authority and regional water authorities.

Openings for work in these departments are described in more detail in Chapters 5 and 6.

Chapter 2

Conservation Issues

Conservation concerns itself with the management and welfare of the natural environment, so the sky is literally the limit for the issues involved. Conservation touches on everything from acid pollution to soil erosion, from African famines to the clearance of tropical forests, from recycling waste to managing a nature reserve on the edge of town.

The main point to emphasise is that conservation, in its short time as a profession, has been through many changes of direction; it is certain to undergo many more, and it may never produce any predictable patterns of employment. A number of issues that have emerged over the past 30 years have changed – some have become more urgent, some less so, and others have been redefined. Conservationists, therefore, must to some extent be opportunist, and respond to the ever-changing circumstances and demands.

For a better understanding of conservation it is essential to look briefly at some of the most urgent and topical issues.

Species Conservation

The natural world is divided into two kingdoms – animals and plants. Conservationists were more interested initially in animals – notably the more attractive mammals and birds because they inspired maximum public support, but reptiles, amphibians, fish, insects and, most importantly, plants have been receiving increasing attention.

Science has so far identified over 1.5 million species of animals and plants, but the inventory is nothing like complete. So much of the natural world remains unexplored, particularly the oceans and the tropical rain forests, and new species are being discovered so frequently that there might be anything between 5 and 10 million species altogether. Over the past 400 years about 40 mammal species and 160 bird species are known to have become extinct. About 1,000 animal species and 25,000 plant species are thought to be threatened, the majority of them by the removal or destruction of their natural habitat. In fact, habitat is being changed so rapidly that the more pessimistic conservationists estimate that extinctions may be occurring at the rate of a species a day, most becoming extinct without even being identified by science.

The importance of animals and plants to the structure of the biosphere and the maintenance of natural systems is obvious, so species conservation (particularly of species in their natural habitat) is a major priority. Conservationists study individual species and their habitat, the status of rare species, captive breeding, population surveys, the control of trade in threatened species, and conservation techniques.

Population

The problem of human population growth was raised as early as the eighteenth century by the English clergyman Thomas Malthus, who warned that there was a limit to the earth's carrying capacity. Thirty or so years ago it became one of the big scares of the 1960s, when pundits like Paul Ehrlich warned of the dangers of a 'population bomb'.

The fear has now lessened, but population growth is still regarded as one of the most crucial of all environmental issues. The world population currently stands at 5 billion, and is expected to increase to more than 6 billion by the end of the century. The most rapid expansion is in Third World countries that can least afford more people.

The problem is not more people *per se*, but the effect they will have on natural resources. A larger population will mean more consumption, and less land available for agriculture, forestry and conservation. So family planning is seen as a major environmental priority.

Third World Development

Many environmental problems are particularly marked in African, Asian and Latin American countries that lack the industrial and economic power to provide their burgeoning populations with adequate fuel, housing, nutrition, health care, sanitation and clean water supplies.

Severely affected by disease, a low life-expectancy, high infant mortality and malnutrition, the world's poor have no time to think about the welfare of the natural environment. In order to survive from day to day, they are usually compelled to put too much pressure on arable land, to encroach on protected natural areas, or to settle in sprawling shanty towns. This degrades the local environment, causes soil erosion, deforestation and the spread of deserts and pollution, and ultimately affects the welfare of the people themselves.

The last 10 years have seen more attention being paid to these problems. Volunteers help Third World communities to become self-sufficient and improve their environmental health standards; planners study the hazards involved in land use and the supply of basic requirements such as food and clean water; environmental scientists examine the problems of species and habitats; and research is undertaken into ways of meeting the needs of the poor while conserving their natural environment.

Energy

Over 90 per cent of our energy supply comes from three non-renewable fossil fuels – oil, coal and gas. Supplies are less of a problem than most people imagine – they are not likely to run out for several generations. The immediate issue to be dealt with is the pollution caused by using fossil fuels. The economic implications of many countries having to rely on imports complicates the matter further.

As a result attention is now being focused on alternative renewable (ie unlimited) energy sources, such as solar power, wind and water power, geothermal energy (from the earth's natural heat), and biomass (from decayed plant or animal matter, of which one product is alcohol).

Chemists, biologists, engineers and geologists are researching these alternative energy sources and their likely environmental implications, and growth in this sector is abundant.

Land Use Planning

The ways in which land is divided up for different uses, and the ways in which it is planned and managed, are central aspects of environmental management. Building a factory without forethought may upset a fragile ecosystem nearby; coastal building development may destroy a valuable wetland or marine ecosystem that supports a nearby fishery; clearing scrub and forest may leave the way open for soil erosion; and so on. With so many demands being made of land, planning is a vital part of conservation.

The Oceans

The oceans cover more than two-thirds of the earth, exercising enormous influence on the structure of the biosphere. All but a narrow coastal strip is beyond national jurisdiction, so the oceans (like the atmosphere and Antarctica) are part of the 'global commons'. As such, there are few controls over how they are used, so they have become the world's rubbish dump, with pollution a problem in many offshore areas, and disagreement about the management of ocean fisheries.

Priority is being given to controlling marine pollution; to studying the effects of exploiting marine resources like fisheries and offshore oil-fields; to learning about the structure of the marine ecosystem; and to conserving threatened marine species, notably whales and seals. The number of marine coastal national parks is increasing, as are the openings for marine scientists.

Pollution

Pollution was given so much publicity and attention during the 1960s and 1970s that anti-pollution laws (in Western Europe and North America at least) have been greatly strengthened. Despite this progress many gaps still remain, new problems, such as those created by the nuclear accident at Chernobyl, have emerged, and there will always be the need to enforce existing laws. In the Third World, where environmental standards are often more lax, pollution is a growing problem, tragically emphasised by the chemical plant explosion and its consequences in Bhopal, India, in 1984.

A large number of environmental scientists are employed in identifying the causes of pollution and coming up with solutions. Two of the most serious international problems are acid pollution (caused by pollutants such as sulphur dioxide and nitrogen oxides reacting with atmospheric water to form diluted acid) and the build-up of carbon dioxide in the atmosphere (caused by the burning of fossil fuels and leading to atmospheric warming, known as the 'greenhouse effect').

As long as we have fossil-fuelled industry and agriculture, there are certain to be by-products and wastes that will become pollutants unless they are correctly processed. This is obviously an area where radical change is imperative.

Forestry

The demand for timber and the clearing of forests for development have led to a worldwide loss of forest cover, often with far-reaching ecological consequences. Forests are the natural habitat of many plant and animal species. They protect topsoil by preventing erosion, avert flooding by absorbing rainwater, and play a vital role in shaping climate.

The need to provide timber for pulp, paper, firewood and building material, coupled with the ecological importance of forests, made forestry one of the first industries to adopt the principles of conservation. But forests still face serious threats (eg from logging and clearance for farming in the Third World, and from acid pollution in the northern hemisphere), and forestry will always need careful and informed management. Therefore the demand for foresters and forest managers will always exist.

Desertification

The semi-arid lands on the edges of deserts are ecologically fragile and susceptible to desertification. A United Nations Environment Programme study has estimated that 6 million hectares a year are reduced to deserts, much of this in developing countries. The Sahelian famine of 1984-85 was largely a result of man-made degradation of the land, and emphasised the urgency of tackling the problem; it preoccupies a host of development agencies and conservation organisations.

Waste

Three things should be considered with regard to waste: first, how to avoid it by using resources such as energy more efficiently; second, how to recycle resources such as food, metal, wood, glass, textiles, plastics, and other commodities which are usually consigned to the waste heap; and finally, how to dispose of wastes that cannot be used again, such as toxic chemicals and radioactive wastes from nuclear power stations.

Recycling reusable wastes lessens demand on the environment and further allows natural resources to be used more sparingly, helping to eliminate pollution. A greater quantity of material is now being recycled, and efforts are being made to extend recycling schemes. Both the theory and the practice of waste management is another growth area, because toxic wastes pose a threat to public health and need to be disposed of carefully.

The government's target of recycling half of all recyclable waste by the year 2000 means that many local authorities are now recruiting recycling officers. Leicester City was created as the first Environment City in 1990; the project includes green show homes, new public transport strategies, low energy use and pollution and local specialist working groups on energy, transport, waste and pollution, food and agriculture. Recycling officers are expected to introduce and implement recycling initiatives, develop existing schemes, locate markets for recycled products and liaise with other bodies on recycling and environmental issues.

Education

There are several facets to education in the context of conservation – formal teaching and training courses at schools and colleges; public information through the promotion of environmental awareness and the use of the mass media (eg the press, radio, television, photography and film); and research aimed at a wider understanding of environmental issues.

This education is currently promoted by the voluntary sector, although the government is becoming increasingly involved. The Inspectorate of Pollutions publishes for industry guidance notes on pollution control. Education and public awareness are dependent on the services of teachers, youth group leaders, information scientists, public relations and press officers, writers, broadcasters, photographers and filmmakers. For further details of opportunities in this area consult Chapters 7 and 9.

Chapter 3

Careers in the Voluntary Sector

Introduction

Conservation owes much to voluntary initiative and relatively little to government action. Like nearly all social reform movements it was born out of the concern of individuals and organisations, and was only given government attention later. Today, although governments take the environment much more seriously than they used to, the jobs of raising money, buying protected areas, breeding threatened species and generating public sympathy still rest with the voluntary sector.

Most British voluntary conservation groups are registered charities. They can be classified broadly into six main groups:

Fund raisers raise money for conservation projects, land purchase, research and education. They spend money according to the advice of experts, and usually help outside agencies and individuals who need financial assistance for conservation work.

Landowners buy up parcels of land, either to preserve important habitats or to establish nature reserves, and employ staff to manage the land.

Wildlife trusts set up, finance and manage facilities for the preservation of threatened species. They may run their own zoos, finance projects in the field or support research work, and usually specialise in anything from otters, butterflies or primates to whole orders, such as birds or mammals.

Pressure groups encourage active campaigning, put pressure on governments to introduce new legislation, and generate public support for their cause. British law does not normally allow them to be registered as charities, so they are usually limited companies.

Naturalists involve amateur and professional naturalists in research and field work on subjects such as ornithology (the study of birds), botany, or herpetology (the study of reptiles).

Practitioners promote practical conservation projects or raise money to carry out specific schemes such as tree-planting, energy conservation, or recycling.

There is much overlap in the work of these voluntary bodies, and most are likely to fall into more than one of the categories. They vary between one-person bodies run from a private home to sprawling national groups with thousands of members, many regional offices, and very large incomes. Administrative costs are nearly always kept to a minimum, so salaries are often relatively low. Employees usually work as part of a team and carry out duties not formally defined in their job specifications.

Openings and Opportunities

These vary according to the organisation. Before approaching a voluntary body you should know the answers to certain basic questions. What kind of organisation is it? What sort of work does it do? How many people does it employ? Does it have regional offices? Does it have openings for people with your particular qualifications? A letter (send an sae for a reply) or a phone call will usually provide the answers. Often the best chance of gaining a permanent job is through working for the organisation as a volunteer.

Voluntary bodies vary in the way they are managed and structured, but usually include the kinds of department described below.

Administration

The bulk of the day-to-day operation of voluntary bodies consists of administration, much of which is routine. Suitably qualified senior managers deal with personnel, financial matters and office management, and are as often appointed for their management skills as for their commitment to conservation.

Working as a secretary is a useful entry into the profession, giving the enterprising person the chance to learn about conservation from the inside, and compete on a strong footing for internal promotion when it arises.

Conservation

Voluntary bodies nearly always employ staff to direct, manage, and carry out their conservation programme. Staff with a background in life sciences are employed to determine conservation policy, manage projects, allocate budgets, advise on campaign planning, provide public information, carry out research and surveys, carry out species protection duties, give advice on educational programmes etc.

Those organisations that buy and own land usually employ full-time and voluntary *wardens* and other staff to manage their reserves. The work may involve breeding threatened species, rehabilitating hurt or injured animals, assessing the threats posed to species or habitats, monitoring the application of environmental laws, or simply running and maintaining a reserve. Wardens need not be scientists, but they should have a proven interest in natural history, enjoy the outdoor life, not have too many domestic commitments, and be prepared to accept basic rates of pay. Vacancies for full-time wardens are always hotly competed for and candidates with experience as voluntary wardens usually have the edge.

Scientific officers usually need relevant qualifications and proven ability to apply their knowledge. Campaigning voluntary bodies usually also employ staff with relevant expertise and experience to present their case to national and local government, statutory bodies, industry, landowners, and any other body whose activities affect the environment. Scientists are usually chosen for these posts, but lawyers are sometimes also needed.

Fund Raising

Every employee of a fund-raising body is helping to raise money in one way or another, but there are usually employees whose sole purpose is to raise money by specific means.

Some charities use commercial promotions where businesses lend their names by advertising the charity and donating a percentage of sales to the organisation. Other charities make direct appeals for donations to commerce, industry, and charitable foundations. Encouraging deeds of covenant from members and prevailing on people to leave money in their wills are two other methods of raising money which are widely employed.

Many voluntary bodies run trading systems whereby they sell products, which are often specially commissioned (eg with a logo or natural history theme), either through a network of shops or through a trading catalogue. The profits from trading are then put into conservation. Signing up members is another form of fund raising which also encourages active involvement in the activities of the charity.

Candidates for fund-raising work should normally have proven commercial experience in fields such as marketing, sales and promotion.

Information and Public Relations

As voluntary bodies rely almost entirely upon public support, public awareness is crucial to their survival. Almost every voluntary body employs at least one or two people, and sometimes a whole department, to process public inquiries, generate press coverage, attract free advertising, write and publish information material, and arrange conferences and exhibitions. Previous experience in advertising, public relations, journalism or information science is an advantage.

Education

Many of the larger voluntary bodies run youth membership groups and education programmes designed to involve teachers, youth leaders, schoolchildren, and youth groups in practical conservation or fund raising. Increasing effort is being put into making sure that conservation is part of school curricula, and conservation education officers try to promote an interest in natural history in children by the use of lectures, film shows and field trips. A desire to work with children is a prerequisite, and teaching experience is usually required.

Regional Staff

Regional offices are run only by the larger voluntary bodies, and can offer openings for people with no experience in conservation although various organisational skills are required. Regional offices are usually smaller versions of the national headquarters, with a small group of people promoting the activities of the body at the local level. This could be fund raising, practical conservation, reserve management, education, or conservation. A knowledge of the local area and the ability to work alone are prerequisites.

To understand the structure of voluntary bodies and to gauge the types of opening available, it is worth looking at a few organisations in more detail. Bear in mind, though, that there are many very different bodies from the ones listed below.

The World Wide Fund for Nature (WWF)

The World Wide Fund for Nature is an international organisation, based in Switzerland and represented in 27 countries (including Britain), which raises money for conservation projects in all parts of the world, designed to ensure the wise and sustainable use of the environment. This involves the protection of renewable nature resources, including wild animals, plants and their habitats.

WWF is a fund-raising charity and has in the last 30 years allocated over £100 million to conservation projects in many parts of the world. A third of all the money raised in each national organisation is retained for use in that country's conservation effort. In the UK it employs a staff of over 200 in its head office in Godalming, Surrey and has a network of 22 regional staff. While full-time openings are limited, there are unrestricted opportunities for voluntary fund-raising work with over 350 local supporters' groups and independent fund-raisers.

The WWF divides its activities into seven main areas:

Finance and administration, consisting of senior management, finance and personnel, and appeals for legacies and deeds of covenant.

Corporate fund raising, which concentrates on raising money through commercial promotions and licensing (where companies agree to donate a percentage of profits from a particular promotion to WWF) and by direct appeals to industry and charitable institutions.

Public relations, which involves establishing and maintaining mutual understanding between an organisation and its public. It involves elements of publicity, marketing, advertising and information.

A *regional network* that employs regional organisers and assistants to create, motivate and support voluntary fund raising at the local level, and to co-ordinate the activities of supporters' groups.

A *consumer fund-raising department* responsible for relations with

WWF members, a direct response section that manages public appeals by mail, and a separate trading company that operates a mail order scheme.

An *education department* responsible for producing material that can be used by teachers in their everyday lessons to enable young people to develop knowledge and values in making informed judgements about environmental issues.

A *conservation department* which provides information and support to all fund-raising efforts in the UK, administers grant aid to conservation projects, and works on specific issues such as marine conservation, forestry policy and so on.

Senior and executive vacancies are advertised nationally, while secretarial and regional staff tend to be recruited locally.

Friends of the Earth (FoE)

FoE is one of the leading environmental pressure groups. It uses the money it raises to fund campaigns to bring key environmental issues to the attention of the public, industry and government. It has a permanent staff in its London headquarters, and also employs permanent staff in some of its local groups around the country.

FoE was founded in 1969 in the United States, and has since spread to more than 35 countries. Each national group is effectively independent of FoE International in that it creates its own structure and campaign methods. The British branch, Friends of the Earth Ltd, was founded in 1971 and divides its work into various campaign areas:

FoE's main campaign areas cover: energy, air pollution and climate change, agriculture and countryside, land use and transport, tropical rainforests, water wastes and toxics and recycling. Some of FoE's most recent successes include mobilising green consumers to persuade the aerosol and fast-food packaging industries to remove ozone-destroying CFCs from their products; establishing pioneering recycling schemes; publicising the location of toxic waste dumps in the UK and reducing the use of tropical hardwoods in Britain.

Particular concerns in the 1990s are the disappearance of the world's rainforests, the increase in air and water pollution and the catastrophic climate changes threatened by global warming.

Apart from the office of the Director and assistants, the headquarters organisation has six other departments:

Campaigns. Managed by the Campaigns Director, each campaign has a staff of senior campaigner and assistants, some responsible for specific issues, and may also have support from senior research officers. Staff also work on international and issues that affect more than one campaign.

Communications. The department is involved in fundraising, campaigning, local group and public communications and is responsible for educational programmes, publications and marketing strategies, including mail order and sales.

Fundraising. Membership subscriptions, donations, sponsorship and fundraising events are handled by the fundraising department, which is responsible for managing and developing the income received by the FoE. A trading section produces the Friends of the Earth catalogue, and is in charge of all products and sales.

Local groups. The support and development of FoE local groups is the responsibility of a team including a local government liaison officer and local groups development officers based in Bristol and Sheffield. A *Project Unit*, including officers in Bristol, Sheffield, Newcastle and Wales, encourages local initiatives such as recycling projects, and is funded by the Department of the Environment.

Finance and administration. These two departments deal with accounts, personnel, office management, computer information, and other normal administrative jobs.

The local groups, of which there are more than 270, are autonomous; they run regional and local campaigns as well as supporting national campaigns. Some groups are large and very active, employing full-time staff and running their own membership schemes. Volunteers can learn a lot about conservation and campaigning.

As most vacancies within the organisation require previous relevant experience, a spell as an FoE could help in getting a permanent post. There are also occasionally temporary jobs of up to three months' duration, normally advertised internally among staff and volunteers. Permanent vacancies are advertised in the *Guardian, The Voice, City Limits* and occasionally *New Scientist*.

The Centre for Alternative Technology

By concentrating on the display of working examples, by educational work, and by the provision of information services, the Centre for Alternative Technology near Machynlleth in Mid-Wales aims to influence people's attitudes towards technology and their own life-style in favour of practices which conserve and protect our planet.

Founded in 1974 and supported by the Alternative Technology Association, the Centre has grown to be a major visitor centre, and now attracts over 85,000 people each year. Several hundreds more, including specialist groups of teachers, architects and others, attend courses on wind power, water power, green living and teaching green.

Among the topics covered by the exhibits and skills at the Centre include wind, solar, biomass and water power, organic horticulture, low-energy building, and electronics for Third World and environmentally sensitive use. Additionally, the Centre runs a bookshop - widely regarded as the most comprehensive alternative technology bookshop in Europe - and a restaurant.

Staff numbers are around 30 permanent workers, plus temporary staff. Additionally, opportunities exist for volunteers to spend periods of a week or six months working with the staff. Write to the Volunteer

Coordinator. Current permanent staff employed at the Centre include engineers, builders, bookshop and restaurant staff, gardeners, publicity and information officers, display and graphic artists, and people to organise courses and visits, and handle finance and general administration.

The Centre publishes a factsheet 'Working in Alternative Technology' and a booklist, both of which would be useful to anyone thinking of working in the field of alternative technology.

Greenpeace

Founded in 1975, Greenpeace campaigns vigorously to protect endangered species and the environment. It has sent its boats into dangerous situations to prevent the killing of whales and seals, nuclear testing in the Pacific and the dumping of toxic waste at sea; it is currently campaigning against global warming, depletion of the ozone layer and air pollution as part of the international Atmosphere and Energy campaign. Salaried posts are advertised in the *Guardian*, specialist journals relevant to particular positions and occasionally other publications. Volunteers for work in the London office at Canonbury Villas, N1 2PN, are encouraged to apply to the reception staff on 071-354 5100. Greenpeace also has a network of local support groups.

Marine Conservation Society

Dedicated to the conservation of marine wildlife and seas, coasts and oceans, the MCS researches and campaigns on marine pollution, conservation and the sustainable use of marine resources. The MCS publishes the *Good Beach Guide* and factsheets on subjects including drift nets, dolphins and whales, energy and global warming, careers (50p each, send sae) and a marine pollution pack (£2.50). In 1991 the Society published proposals for an Integrated Coastal Zone Management system for the UK. It has recently opened a Scottish office with a special interest in fish farming and marine conservation in Scotland. The Society's headquarters is at Ross-on-Wye, Herefordshire; staff numbers are small; voluntary helpers become involved with projects such as Norwich Union Coastwatch UK, Seasearch (underwater survey work calls for experienced divers), basking shark and marine curio trade surveys.

Whale and Dolphin Conservation Society

An international organisation, the Whale and Dolphin Conservation Society has offices in Bath and Lincoln, Massachusetts. Working for the conservation, welfare and appreciation of cetaceans (the collective name for whales, dolphins and porpoises), it was founded by Dr Roger Payne, one of the discoverers of the humpback whale 'songs' and pioneer of the *Save the Whale* movement. An aim is to promote public education and awareness through their own publications and the media and monitor the proceedings of the International Whaling Commission. In the UK, non-scientific permanent administration staff number about ten, full and part time; three marine biologists are based at Boston, USA. Posts are advertised in the local press, the *Guardian*, *Independent* and *New Scientist*.

British Trust for Conservation Volunteers (BTCV)

BTCV involves individuals and communities in practical environmental projects. From working only on national nature reserves, its remit has now expanded to include education and amenity work in the countryside. Each year over 50,000 volunteers are equipped and trained to carry out environmental work on over 15,000 sites across the countryside, with projects ranging from the protection of wildlife habitats to the improvement of access to the countryside. Opportunities for voluntary work in the environmental field include spending between 3 and 12 months working as a voluntary field officer in one of BTCV's residential centres, volunteer involvement on a conservation working holiday, training as a leader to work on residential conservation projects and working at weekends with affiliated local groups (over 600). BTCV is one of the partners in UK2000, involving people of all ages in practical conservation, from drystone walling to nature reserve management, pond clearing to working in tree nurseries. Conservation Practice, a subsidiary of BTCV, promotes training and develops enterprise in environmental projects.

BTCV has a permanent staff of over 175, working in around 75 offices throughout the country. Most work at regional or local level, promoting the involvement of volunteers in the projects. The most important position is that of *field officer*, with a range of responsibilities according to locality: creating a wildlife garden in an inner-city area, or dealing with the problems of tourist pressures on footpaths in a National Park. Their work includes setting up training courses, organising working holidays, running projects for unemployed or retired people and involving schoolchildren in environmental work. Most field officers have a degree background in environmental studies and several years' experience in practical conservation work, often as a BTCV volunteer.

RSNC: The Wildlife Trusts Partnership

Also a UK2000 partner and formerly known as the Royal Society for Nature Conservation, the Wildlife Trusts Partnership is concerned with all aspects of wildlife protection. It is a partnership of 47 Wildlife Trusts, 50 Urban Wildlife Groups, and WATCH, the junior wing. Together they protect over 2000 sites covering more than 56,000 hectares. The partnership has a total of 500 full- and part-time staff. Each Trust has between 4 and 40 permanent members of staff. As well as graduates with degrees in subjects such as biological sciences, ecology and conservation, and those with experience in voluntary work, there are opportunities for those with PR and marketing skills.

Other voluntary organisations include:

The Council for the Preservation of Rural England, concerned with the care and improvement of the whole of England's countryside and not simply particular features or elements in it; it has 44 county branches.

The National Trust, which protects places of natural beauty or historical interest, and employs many specialists with professional qualifications and experience and also gives Youth Training to school leavers in amenity horticulture, forestry and countryside management. The Trust provides training opportunities for around 36 school leavers a year through its 15 Regional Offices in England and Wales. Specialist staff include Land Agents; archaeological, forestry, nature conservation and horticultural advisory staff; gardeners, forestry staff and wardens; architects and building and conservation staff.

The Civic Trust, concerned with conserving historic towns and cities, and the economic and social regeneration of urban areas through conservation, including the restoration of canal and rail corridors.

Case Studies

Alan works in the regional office of a national conservation charity.

> I actually discovered conservation by accident. I read geography at university, not knowing what I wanted to do after graduation, and during a vacation a friend of mine took me along to a two-week work camp on a nature reserve. I suppose I'd always been sympathetic to the aims of conservation, but my interest was really aroused in those two weeks by meeting and talking to people working in conservation. I subsequently worked on several reserves and conservation projects at weekends and during holidays, and on one project met the regional officer who offered me a job. The fact that I had practical conservation experience and knew a fair bit about the charity I now work for were probably the deciding factors, although the geography degree was useful.

At first Alan was given largely routine and menial duties, but then the regional officer moved on to the head office, and Alan was offered his present job.

> It's a good job for the time being, but I can't see myself staying here for ever. The regional office is a miniature version of head office, the difference being that I'm involved in every aspect of the job and I'm effectively my own boss. If anything, you tend to be completely forgotten by head office. The work is mostly fund raising, generating local publicity, and giving talks to schools and societies. It means a lot of travel, a lot of work with the public, acting as a one-man information service, and even doing the occasional newspaper or radio interview. The pay isn't that good and the hours are long, but there is a lot of satisfaction in seeing the amount of money you're raising and watching your membership figures climbing slowly.

Alan's future plans are to pick up as much experience as possible and then move up to head office (or another charity) and become more involved in information and conservation policy.

Fiona works in the national office of an environmental pressure group. She left school when she was 16 and did a variety of jobs before taking a secretarial course and moving to London to work as a secretary. After two years of temping she was sent to the pressure group for a one-month stint that turned into a permanent job.

I took a big drop in salary, but I'd heard a lot about the group and got very interested in what it was doing. Most of the time I'm a jack of all trades – we all are – but I work mostly on the publications side. The nicest thing about working with the group is that there is no real hierarchy and everyone shares the work. In the past year I have helped organise a rally in Hyde Park and a pop concert, helped start up five glass and paper recycling schemes, and I've just been put in charge of liaising with the various celebrities who support us. I'm learning a lot of skills as I go along – you just have to, because you have to pay your own way and not be a passenger. The biggest problems are the low pay, the erratic hours, and the cramped office space. You also sometimes feel you are a bit on the fringes of the real world, but the sense of doing something socially useful makes up for all that.

Chapter 4

Resource Management

Introduction

In recent years the increasing demand for natural resources has given rise to a need for extensive and thorough planning procedures, particularly in the densely populated countries of the industrialised north, and there is now a variety of career options for anyone wanting to become involved in this area of work.

In this chapter some of the more important options in resource management planning are considered.

Town and Country Planning

An increasing population and growing pressures on land have heightened the need for effective planning systems in recent decades. Countryside planning is of particular interest to anyone wanting a career in resource conservation. The conflicting demands of agriculture, amenity, recreation and conservation have to be met, and the countryside planner has much influence over the overall outcome.

The structure of planning in the United Kingdom was laid out in the 1947 Planning Act, significantly revised in 1971, which required planning authorities to prepare development plans for the allocation of land for roads, housing, industry, open space, agriculture, conservation and other uses. Private and public development was also controlled to fit in with the overall scheme for the country, with the result that the UK now has a comprehensive planning structure. It has not always been ideal, but it provides the rule against which people with conflicting demands can measure the allocation of land.

About 60 per cent of the openings for planners are in local government. The Department of the Environment is the central government body which supervises planning. It publishes the policies of the government, issues guidance on practices and procedures, commissions research, and provides local planners with information. At the regional level, county councils (regional councils in Scotland) draw up broad strategic plans for the development of each county, based on careful surveys of the county's economic and physical resources.

At local level, district councils prepare local plans, which go into more detail than the county structure plan, and also oversee development control by dealing with applications to develop or change the use of land. This is the area that directly affects all our lives, and most directly affects the quality of the environment. Plans and changes at every level must in turn be subject to public inquiries, particularly if there are objections.

Outside central and local government there are opportunities for planners in statutory bodies such as the Countryside Commission, water authorities, national park planning authorities and development corporations. There has recently been a growth in the number of independent professional planning consultants. Private consultancies are often commissioned to work on special schemes for local government, but otherwise operate mostly with institutions such as universities, or work on private sector development schemes. There is expected to be an increasing amount of work abroad, especially in the EC from 1992.

What the Job Entails
Whether working for the public authorities or the private sector, the job of the planner is to help in preparing development plans, which involves carrying out all the necessary research, survey and consultation work in the field and working with experts in related areas. Planners work as part of a team, and might be asked to work on a variety of jobs, from working out population trends to improving the environment by planting trees or reclaiming derelict land. The plan could be a general one for an entire county, a specific local one for a country park or a coastal development, or an environmental scheme within a small area. Planners have to consult the public, politicians, officials, industrialists, financiers and technical experts concerned with conservation and development.

Qualities Required
Planners must be able to work together in teams and with experts and advisers in different fields. They must have a great interest in the environment, and understand the needs of the community, and must be able to communicate their ideas and plans to all the people with whom they come in contact. They should be broad-minded, logical, willing to listen to and take advice from others, able to back up their ideas with careful research, have the self-assurance to back up their decisions, and be able to cope with the many frustrations that come with the job.

Qualifications
Membership of the Royal Town Planning Institute (RTPI) is the recognised professional qualification for town planners in the UK, and this is accepted in many other countries as well. Candidates have to satisfy the Institute's academic and practical training requirements, and must have had two years' practical experience. About 95 per cent of entrants enter planning via a recognised course at a school of planning, university, polytechnic or college, and can become student members of the Institute. There are undergraduate courses for school leavers, or postgraduate courses for graduates with relevant first degrees, usually in architecture, surveying, engineering, geography, economics or sociology. The alterna-

tive to a college course is to study at home on the RTPI distance learning course.

Openings and Prospects

Job prospects for qualified planners are reasonably healthy at present but do fluctuate with the economic climate and the level of local and central government spending. The RTPI currently has over 15,000 members and student members. The work of planners is changing, with many people now involved in areas such as economic development, conservation and tourism, as well as the more traditional areas of development control and local planning. It can also be useful to back up a qualification in planning with skills in related fields such as architecture and surveying.

Forestry

Forestry is the art and science of managing forests, which includes everything from raising seedlings and transplants in nurseries, to felling and transporting wood, planting and tending new forest plantations, managing woodland for recreation and amenity, and conserving the forest environment and its wildlife.

Forests are a renewable natural resource and, as such, need careful planning and management. Trees not only provide timber for everything from paper to furniture, building material, fuel and fencing, but also have a vital ecological role. They provide a natural habitat for plant and animal life and have an important bearing on soil cover, water retention, wind and climate. New plantings of coniferous trees make more allowance for wildlife and conservation of landscape than previous plantations, with less wholesale cutting down of large areas, a greater mix of trees of different ages, and even natural regeneration by wind-carried seed, plus unplanted areas as wildlife habitat. Trees are an important feature of the landscape, particularly in towns where they help to soften the built environment.

The art of raising and tending trees is old, but the science of forest management is relatively new. It involves planning, predicting timber demands, controlling felling and replanting, ecological management and marketing. It is central to national resource policy. For instance, Britain was once almost entirely covered in woodland, but now has 8 per cent forest cover, less than any country in Europe except Ireland and the Netherlands.

There are 2 million hectares of productive woodlands in the UK, 888,000 hectares of which is managed by the Forestry Commission. The rest is divided between private forest estates, private woodlands and woodland owned by timber merchants.

What the Job Entails

Forestry at the moment employs about 18,000 people, working mainly in the Forestry Commission and the private estates. Others work in forest management companies, harvesting companies and wood processing industries. The Forestry Commission's structured employment pattern contrasts with that of the private sector, where career development depends on the individual employer.

Private estates vary in size from less than 40 to more than 200 hectares, and employ some or all of the following staff:

Land agents (*factors* in Scotland) put the policy of the owner into practice; they must be members of the Royal Institution of Chartered Surveyors or the Incorporated Society of Valuers and Auctioneers. *Forest officers* are given charge of the forestry section. *Foresters* are responsible for planning the annual programme of forestry work, supervising and training forest workers, and controlling the progress of work schemes and specialist activities such as research and wildlife conservation. *Foremen* oversee work parties. *Forest workers* (or *woodmen*) are the craftsmen and team workers, and are trained for a variety of jobs from clearing and weeding to planting, servicing and operating machinery, using chain saws, applying fertilisers, supervising nurseries and pruning and thinning trees. *Rangers* and *wardens* manage and control wildlife, maintain campsites and recreational facilities, and guide visitors around forest reserves. Other workers operate machines, run sawmills, and undertake other skilled and unskilled jobs.

Qualities Required
Most foresters are united by an interest in, and understanding of, the needs of wildlife and the countryside, and of the forestry industry. They live mainly in the country or small towns and villages, and must enjoy the outdoor life, be able to work alone while fitting into the needs of the industry at large, and be able to express and communicate the essentials of forestry to administrators, planners, farmers, sportsmen and the public.

Qualifications
These vary according to the type of work, but all except forest workers and woodmen need specialist training. This could be basic craft training for new entrants provided by the Forestry Commission and Forestry Training Council, or a diploma or degree in forest science and management.

Openings and Prospects
The number of people employed in forestry has decreased, partly because of the introduction of new methods of making the industry more efficient and productive in the face of overseas competition. However, numbers have now stabilised.

In the UK there are opportunities in local government service, in national parks, in voluntary land-owning bodies such as the National Trust, in commerce and industry, in teaching and research, and in private forests and with the Forestry Commission. There are also many opportunities of various kinds overseas, on short-term contracts in the

Third World or in permanent posts in countries such as Canada, Australia and New Zealand.

The Water Industry

The demand for water for domestic, industrial and commercial consumption has been increasing steadily in recent years, and even in a country with a normally high rainfall, such as the UK, water shortages have become more frequent. The importance of managing and conserving water resources, the need to treat waste water and control pollution, and the importance of flood protection led to a review of the organisation of the water industry.

The main employers in England and Wales are now 10 private water service companies and the National Rivers Authority (see Chapter 5).

In Scotland, there is a different two-tier system with nine regional councils divided into 53 district councils. Purification is handled by seven area groups responsible for the quantity and quality of water discharged into rivers and coastal waters.

What the Job Entails

Like all natural resources, water is governed by limits, and careless use will lead to shortages and deterioration in the quality of rivers, lakes, dams and reservoirs. Water often needs to be recycled to bolster supply, which involves treatment to remove effluent and sewage.

RWAs and their Scottish equivalents are responsible for forecasting water demand, developing new sources, flood forecasting, hydrometry, storing and supplying water, land drainage, and fisheries. They are also responsible for the conservation of water as a resource, the control of river pollution, and nature conservation. They employ biologists and geologists, specialists in fisheries management, civil engineers, hydrologists, and a variety of administrative staff and skilled and unskilled workers.

Openings and Prospects

Although openings for biologists and water pollution control scientists are still fairly limited, the RWAs are showing more interest in graduate recruitment. There are also openings in advisory, supervisory, technical and managerial positions in water resources, distribution and supply and treatment areas.

The Energy Industry

Energy is the backbone of our industrial and technological way of life. It provides light, warmth and power, cooks our food, fuels our transport systems and industries and, above all, makes the existence of life on earth possible. Over the centuries we have generated energy from a wide variety of sources (everything from charcoal to nuclear power) and have created extensive industries to extract and manage our energy needs.

At the moment all but 8 per cent of our energy comes from three sources: oil, coal and natural gas. They are all fossil fuels and are all non-renewable. This means that one day they will run out. The result is that we are now beginning to use energy more efficiently and intensively by cutting down on waste, and are also investigating new sources such as solar, wind, wave, bioenergy and geothermal energy.

Bioenergy covers a variety of technologies, including the production of methane from waste and the growing of energy-crops, and is the sector expected to expand the most.

Large-scale wind turbines and wind farms linked to a national grid have been developed by large construction companies, and by GEC and British Aerospace, and the construction of tidal barrages is being considered as a way of generating electricity. It is also possible that shipyards could be used to manufacture wave energy converters. Large firms such as Calor, Pilkington and Philips are also interested in wave power and solar energy. Solar power, bioenergy, energy conservation and heat pumps are all in the research and development stage, both in university research groups and with smaller engineering companies, many of whom are already manufacturing water turbines and small wind turbines for domestic and agricultural use.

Energy conservation is a growth area for jobs, with 5,000 to 10,000 jobs in the renewable energy field, including hydroelectric plants, plus energy conservation work. Energy managers are employed by both industrial companies and local authorities to reduce the use of energy; it is their job to make cash savings, challenge accepted practices and propose feasible alternatives, and prevent detrimental effects on the environment. A list of manufacturers and installers of renewable energy equipment is available from the Centre for Alternative Technology.

Warwick University has an AT-specific degree course: Engineering Design for Appropriate Technology (EDAT). Some science-based degrees contain AT options, such as the Society and Technology degree at Middlesex University, and special energy or environmental degrees at colleges, including Napier University, Edinburgh, the University of East London, and Reading University. Many of those employed in the field of renewable energy are architects or engineers. Information about suitable energy courses and jobs are given in the NATTA (Network for Alternative Technology and Technology Assessment) newsletter; details are available from NATTA Energy and Environmental Research Unit, Faculty of Technology, The Open University, Milton Keynes MK7 6AA.

Landscape Architecture

Landscape architecture is a small, young, but fast-growing profession with about 3,400 professionally qualified members and the demand exists for many more. The career offers excellent prospects and considerable job satisfaction to anyone with an interest in the natural environment.

Landscape architecture consists of planning and designing open spaces. Landscape architects can both protect existing features and help nature to return to otherwise sterile urban locations.

What the Job Entails
The landscape architect analyses and resolves the demands made on open spaces, and uses the spaces to best effect. This might involve restoring derelict land, or landscaping a new town scheme, a housing or industrial estate, shopping precinct, golf course, marina, cemetery, a stretch of motorway, a public park, or a private garden. Each design has to consider the ecological, functional, aesthetic and management aspects of the scheme.

The landscape architect usually takes a brief from a client, carries out a detailed survey of the site, and then designs a scheme that draws on the advice of ecologists, planners, architects and engineers. Once a contractor has been appointed, the landscape architect works on the site to oversee the implementation of the scheme.

There are three specialist areas within the profession:

Landscape architects, trained in design as well as technical skills, supervise the scheme on the drawing board and on site. *Landscape scientists* are especially concerned with environmental factors and have qualifications in a natural science plus expertise in ecology, soil science, geology, hydrology or plant or animal biology. *Landscape managers* have a background in horticulture, forestry or agriculture and are responsible for the long-term care, development and management of the scheme. Landscape constructors may also be on site. Their skills range from unskilled manual tasks to skilled management, and combine a knowledge of horticulture and agriculture with basic building practice.

Qualities Required
Landscape architects should have an instinct to preserve and conserve, and should be deeply concerned about the natural environment. The job demands an interest in both art and science, and in people and the way they relate to the natural environment. Landscape architects also need to be physically fit, and prepared to spend most of their time out of doors.

Qualifications
Membership of the Landscape Institute is the recognised professional qualification for landscape architects in the UK. To be eligible for associate membership of the Institute, candidates must have two years' work experience and pass the Institute's professional practice exam, having successfully completed a course at one of the recognised schools of landscape architecture in landscape architecture or landscape management. There are no specific courses in landscape science, but some courses, such as the MSc in Conservation at University College London and the MSc in Ecology at Aberdeen University, are appropriate.

Openings and Prospects
Landscape architects work either in private practice or for government, industry, development corporations, or planning departments, and are commissioned to work both on private and public land. As the profession grows, so the number of openings will increase. Private practice currently

offers most of the opportunities, but government and public and private organisations are taking on more landscape architects. There are also openings overseas, either working on projects given to British consultancies or working with overseas consultancies.

Surveying

Surveying as a profession covers a wide field of interests, including everything from quantity surveying to estate agency work, and also involving a number of public and private bodies responsible for resource management. Many surveyors help to determine planning and development policy.

Chartered surveyors specialise in matters relating to land, property and buildings, and concern themselves with the management, development, and financial operation of aspects of land use. All surveyors are trained in the basic professional skills needed to carry out their job effectively, after which they specialise. For environmental managers and conservationists, there are the following main areas of interest:

Rural practice surveyors can be involved in a range of local responsibilities, including managing country estates and agricultural businesses as land agents, and advising landowners and farmers, or other countryside interests, including organisations concerned with conservation and the rural environment. They advise on forestry and the care of woodlands used as amenities or as commercial ventures, and on development schemes for agriculture and recreation. Through their advice to local authorities and others they can influence UK and EC policy on the development of the environment.

Planning and development surveyors stay with major projects, such as housing schemes, from the first planning stages to final completion; they prepare and obtain planning permission, and raise finance. A project such as a housing scheme would include the analysis of existing residential accommodation against population forecasts.

Land surveyors use advanced technology such as satellite positioning systems and laser alignment devices to collect information about natural and man-made features of the landscape. This helps in deciding where building and other major projects such as roads, bridges and housing estates should be sited.

Hydrographic surveyors gather information to manage the marine environment, including the preparation of charts and the dredging of ports and channels.

Marine resource management surveyors work in ocean management, which includes the development of sources of ocean energy – wave, tidal, ocean thermal energy conversion and ocean wind energy – as well as pollution, recreation, coastal engineering, land reclamation, mineral extraction and fisheries. Surveyors in this speciality would work closely with marine biologists to assess the ecology of the ocean, monitor changes caused by marine activities and recommend solutions.

Qualities Required
Surveyors are members of a profession that demands a high degree of social responsibility. They need the knowledge and breadth of outlook to understand how resources need developing and planning, and the flair for seeing and understanding all the social, aesthetic, financial, economic and legal aspects of the job. This means working as part of a team of experts in different fields, and being able to contribute to collective decisions. Land and hydrographic surveying demand a high degree of technical and mathematical ability.

Qualifications
School leavers can qualify as surveyors either by taking and passing a recognised university or polytechnic course, or by working in a surveyor's office as a student member of the Royal Institution of Chartered Surveyors through part-time or day-release study. Candidates are then assessed for the Test of Professional Competence, after two years' approved experience. A minimum of five GCSE/GCE passes, including two at A level, and passes in maths and English language or literature, are needed for entry to courses leading to the Institution's professional exams.

Openings and Prospects
Vacancies in the areas of most interest to conservationists and environmental managers tend to be the most difficult to come by. Candidates usually have to pick up experience in a related area of surveying while awaiting suitable openings. Because so many surveyors are employed in government service, the frequency of openings tends to fluctuate with the economic climate and level of government spending.

Park and Recreation Management

As an increasing number of people have more leisure time, so the demand for better recreational facilities grows, and both national and local authorities are putting more energy into meeting this demand. Working in parks and recreation involves providing a variety of outdoor and indoor facilities, most of which are designed to increase people's enjoyment of natural features. The work might mean managing and planning local town or city parks, woodland, estates, playing fields, cemeteries, crematoria, allotments, and almost any site designed for public recreation.

An imaginative manager could turn a barren piece of land, in an unprepossessing urban area, into a haven for wildlife, or carefully convert a cemetery into an attractive local nature reserve. The job incorporates aspects of horticulture, arboriculture, landscape design, construction and conservation.

The 11 national parks in England and Wales, including the Broads, are privately owned, mainly by farmers and landowners and the people who live and work within the park areas, and administered by local boards and county councils. Farmers and landowners are encouraged and helped to carry out work that contributes to the conservation of the landscape and wildlife. Landowners include the National Trust, and there are also some areas managed by the Forestry Commission and wildlife habitats protected by voluntary organisations such as English Nature. Conservation in the parks is the responsibility of park rangers, or wardens, with help from volunteers – who may use this as a route into a permanent job.

The members of the Association of Countryside Rangers, who work in the National Parks and other conservation areas, are involved in the daily management and conservation of sites and larger areas, and in environmental education (including guided walks for visitors). Over half work for local authorities; other employers, apart from the national parks authorities, are the National Trust, the Woodland Trust, county naturalists trusts and English Nature.

What the Job Entails
There are three levels of career in park and recreation management: professional, technical and craft. All are interrelated, and there are possibilities for promotion within and between the different levels.

Craft work demands a variety of different skills that can be learned, either on the job or on a three-year course that involves working and taking day-release classes at colleges of further education. The work involves anything from using and maintaining tools and machinery to laying out horticultural features, cultivating plants, maintaining trees, building paths and drains and constructing special public facilities.

Technical work involves the same duties at a more specialised level, and *professional* posts are reserved for those with appropriate qualifications and management abilities.

Qualities Required
A love of, and understanding for, the needs of nature are essential, as is an interest in meeting the recreational needs of the community. Members of the profession work as a team to meet those needs and to maintain minimum standards on each scheme. An interest in horticulture (the cultivation of plants), arboriculture (the cultivation of trees) and conservation are all part of the job.

Qualifications
The body that promotes and oversees the profession is the Institute of Leisure and Amenity Management, which promotes education in the field and sets professional standards. Membership of the Institute is the recognised professional qualification. Technical posts call for candidates with four (appropriate) GCSEs, or at least one science A level, who may be eligible for specialised training in amenity horticulture or a technical subject such as landscape and horticultural technology.

Candidates for professional posts usually need at least four GCSEs and one A level, and to spend time as trainees attending day-release classes, followed by further training in amenity horticulture. Candidates with two or more A levels may go on to read horticulture at university and work in the service during vacations.

Openings and Prospects

As most jobs in park and recreation management are currently offered by local authorities responsible for parks, recreation, amenity and leisure, so opportunities vary with the policies and budgets of each authority. There are also occasional vacancies with the national parks authorities. Although work for local authorities is subject to competitive tendering, most of the work is carried out by the authorities' own recreation and leisure departments, rather than by private contractors.

Working in Industry

Industrial technology gave us the means to exploit the earth's resources over the past 200 years. However, many environmental problems have been caused by unrestrained and unplanned industrial development. Perhaps the most obvious bad side-effect has been pollution.

The situation is now changing: the tightening up of legislation, the requirements of central and local government, and a greater awareness of the need for minimum standards of environmental health have combined to make industry take its environmental obligations more seriously in recent years.

While there has been a rise in the number of environmental planners and scientists employed by industry, openings are still limited and it is difficult to make any generalisations or firm forecasts. Many industries have been able to 'clean up' by tightening up their existing policies and by making their workforces aware of the issues. They have not found a need to employ environmental specialists. Other industries have employed ecologists and biologists to monitor anti-pollution measures, the effects of industry on local ecosystems, and the needs of resource planning. Much of this is supported by intensified public relations programmes.

One company might be looking for extremely well-qualified specialists, such as biochemists, plant ecologists, microbiologists, or botanists, to work on specific projects. Another may do no more than consider applicants with environmental science qualifications on a par with other general applicants. Yet another company may give preference to environmental scientists for general vacancies where their expertise could be a bonus.

Because there are no hard and fast rules, looking for openings in industry is a matter of assessing which organisations are most likely to employ environmentalists, and to approach each one individually. The number of openings in this area is likely to increase especially for those qualified in chemistry, botany and biology.

There are also opportunities in large companies and consultancy groups for those with experience and qualifications in ecology and the environment, to assess and advise on the impact of projects such as civil engineering and construction works.

Working in Agriculture

The natural vegetation of the British Isles at one time was woodland, but for the past 1,000 years at least it has been gradually replaced by agriculture and the patchwork quilt of fields and hedgerows that now characterises our landscape. More than two-thirds of our land is now farmed, and agriculture employs nearly half a million people.

So while it is not surprising that agricultural policy has enormous influence on the quality of our natural environment, it offers very few openings for conservationists and environmental planners. Nevertheless, this apparent lack of opportunity has not stopped suitably qualified environmental scientists and planners from working in agriculture, although they have to compete for vacancies with agricultural scientists. Experience in farm work, and qualifications in soil science, biology, horticulture or a similar area, are normal requirements for a job in this field. Agricultural research is another likely avenue for those with relevant specialist skills, and a few opportunities exist for work on the environmental consequences of agricultural policy and research into more efficient and ecologically sound agricultural methods.

For those without skills or qualifications, manual work on farms leading to farm management work offers the chance to supervise and plan the running of a farm, and to make decisions on how the land is used.

Under the Countryside Stewardship Scheme, developed with the Countryside Commission, English Nature, and English Heritage, farmers and other landowners receive incentives to help them combine commercial land management with conservation; the scheme has five target landscapes of chalk and limestone grassland, lowland heath, waterside landscapes, coastal areas and uplands. Farmers can also apply for the Countryside Premium, which provides incentives to farmers to manage set-aside land for the benefit of wildlife and the landscape.

The Farming and Wildlife Advisory Group employs approximately 45 Farm Conservation Advisers who give advice to farmers on: whole-farm and partial conservation plans; conserving or planting hedges and hedgerow trees; making and maintaining ponds; improving field margins, tracks and roadside verges; conserving wetlands, scrub, rough grass and old woodland; planting trees in new woodland and tree groups. They also give talks, run courses and guided farm walks and attend county shows, meetings and conferences.

One area of agriculture that is growing is organic farming, based on crop rotation, non-chemical pest and disease control, the recycling of nutrients and a healthy soil structure – as an alternative to intensive, chemically based production methods. The total acreage under organic production is increasing at around 5 per cent per month.

The British Organic Farmers and the Organic Growers Association organises one-day training courses, produces technical booklets and has a library and resource centre at the Organic Food and Farming Centre, 86

Colston Street, Bristol. Some agricultural colleges now have short course modules dealing with organic farming and non-intensive methods of food production within existing courses. The Soil Association also provides information about education and training opportunities in organic agriculture; a list of courses approved by the Association is available from the Organic Food and Farming Association, address as above (send sae).

Other organisations involved in organic farming are the Organic Advisory Service, Elm Farm Research Centre, Hamstead Marshall, Nr Newbury, Berkshire RG15 0HR; the Bio-Dynamic Agricultural Association, Woodman Lane, Clent, Stourbridge, West Midlands DY9 9PX; the Henry Doubleday Research Association, Ryton-on-Dunsmore, Coventry CV8 3LG, and the Centre for Alternative Technology. For practical experience, Working Weekends on Organic Farms arrange work in exchange for meals and accommodation; details from WWOOF, 19 Bradford Road, Lewes, Sussex BN7 1RB.

A career in agriculture is worth considering, but it is up to the individual to create the openings and to acquire the right training – there are few precedents to use for guidance.

Chapter 5

Working for the Government

Introduction

Most environmentalists in the UK would tend to define British political philosophy as essentially unsympathetic to their cause, although much progress has been made in the formulation of environmental laws, controls on planning and the protection of species and habitats. The creation of the Department of the Environment in 1970 was a significant step, and other departments have since gradually adopted new policies in favour of environmental management and protection.

This has given rise to an expansion in the number of job opportunities for planners and environmental scientists. Most of these openings fall within the normal Civil Service structure, and appointments are made by individual government departments (look for job advertisements in the press). To obtain such an opening usually means first joining the Civil Service in a general capacity, and then moving to a relevant department as soon as possible. Administrative, scientific and research posts provide the most likely options for conservationists.

Openings for School Leavers

If you have GCSEs or A levels and no specialist knowledge, clerical and executive posts provide the main point of entry. The first rung on the ladder is the *administrative assistant*, whose work involves keeping records, sorting, filing, and answering public inquiries. There are no age restrictions for entry, but two acceptable GCSE passes, including English language, are normally required or candidates can take a written test.

The next step up is the *administrative officer*, who handles the incoming correspondence of the department, helps the public, either on the phone or over the counter, and keeps records and accounts. There are no age limits for entry, which is either by promotion from administrative assistant, or by successful applications from newcomers with five acceptable GCSE passes, including English language or a written test.

Executive officer posts are the most responsible of the administrative posts, which involve the application of departmental policy, managing the work of administrative assistants and officers, and working directly with the public. There are opportunities for specialist training. An applicant needs to be under 52 years old, and have two A levels and three

GCSEs, or their equivalent. One of the passes must be in English language. Promotion beyond this point is normally to *higher executive officer*; entrants need two A levels and four years' experience.

School leavers can also apply for vacancies as *assistant scientific officers* to support research and project teams. Applicants should have A levels or four acceptable GCSEs, including English language and a maths or science subject. Opportunities exist for specialisation and advancement into preferred areas of work.

All these staff are recruited locally by individual departments.

Openings for Graduates

There are opportunities in the Civil Service for graduates with both general and specialist or professional qualifications. Administration is the main point of entry for the specialists and includes policy planning, the drafting of legislation, or the management of executive programmes.

Administration trainees spend two years at that level, combining their work with training at the Civil Service College. They should have the practical intelligence needed to assess and deal with problems they encounter, be able to work in a team, and be able to express themselves clearly. Applicants should be under 26 and should have a degree with at least second class honours. Promotion is to *higher executive officer*, *Grade 7, Grade 6*, and so on.

For those with at least a second class degree in an appropriate specialised field, there are opportunities in research areas. *Research officers* study the impact of government policy, and provide information upon which to base future policy. The Resource and Planning Group is particularly interesting because it studies policy in relation to the allocation of resources and the environment. Applicants should normally be aged under 28 and be qualified in geography, agricultural economics, economics, economic geography, or a related field. Promotion is to *senior research officer*.

Scientists are needed for advisory services, and to carry out research and development. Applicants should have an appropriate degree or equivalent qualification.

Vacancies for graduates are usually advertised nationally by the Recruitment and Assessment Services Agency, or the relevant government department.

Relevant Government Departments

While environmental specialists may be employed on a full-time or consultancy basis at one time or another by almost all government departments, the majority of openings are in the following departments.

The Department of the Environment (DoE)

Despite its name, nature conservation and resource planning are only one part of the work of the DoE. The 'Environment' in its name refers to people's living environment, and includes areas such as housing, new towns policy, and local government.

The Department also has responsibilities in planning, development control, inner city renewal, countryside affairs, pollution control and water resources. It has two headquarters offices in London and Bristol, and nine regional offices. There are five divisions of particular interest:

Planning. The DoE oversees regional and local planning policy, and is one of the largest employers of qualified planners. The headquarters of the Planning Inspectorate is in Bristol.

Royal Parks and *Historic Royal Palaces Agency.* Staff working in the Royal Parks are employed by private contractors. They include qualified horticulturalists, gardens, birdkeepers and gamekeepers; among the 350 staff in the Royal Palaces Agency there are gardeners and specialists in conservation. The DoE is also responsible for 'listing' buildings with special architectural or historic merit and giving grants to, and monitoring, bodies such as English Heritage and voluntary organisations.

Countryside and Wildlife. The DoE has a policy responsibility for the conservation and enhancement of the countryside. This includes recreation and the resolution of possible conflicts where varied demands are made of land. The Department employs some part-time specialist staff for posts such as Wildlife Inspectors. It also sponsors and works with statutory agencies such as the Countryside Commission, English Nature and the Scottish and Welsh conservancy bodies (see Chapter 6).

Pollution control. The DoE has responsibility within central government for policy on most aspects of pollution control and co-ordinates policy on the remainder. Her Majesty's Inspectorate of Pollution, part of the DoE, exercises direct control over air pollution from certain processes and the handling of radioactive substances. It also advises local authorities on the exercise of their functions in respect of air pollution and the disposal of waste to land.

Along with the National Rivers Authority (see below), HMIP will form part of the new Environment Agency, which will take over the regulation of waste disposal. HMIP is also responsible for the new system of Integrated Pollution Control, controlling emissions of all kinds from the industries of fuel and power, waste disposal, minerals, chemicals, metals and other industries including paper pulp manufacture, timber processes and animal and plant material treatment. HMIP's staff is expected to grow from 260 to around 400 over the next few years to cope with its extra responsibilities. A Pollution Inspector must have an honours degree in chemistry, chemical engineering, mechanical engineering, physics, environmental science or other relevant discipline, or appropriate professional qualifications and experience.

National Rivers Authority. The NRA, which will be merged into the Environment Agency, employs around 6,500 people and is made up of ten regions based on the river catchment areas of England and Wales. The principal functions of the authority are: water quality; water resources;

flood defence; freshwater fisheries; conservation; recreation and navigation. The rivers, lakes, estuaries and coastal waters protected by the NRA include Sites of Special Scientific Interest (SSSIs) and wildlife habitats, with corridors and wilderness areas in towns and cities as well as farmland. The Authority is also responsible for conserving archaeological features and historic buildings. Ecologist and Conservation Officers survey river or coastal areas, liaising with the engineers responsible for engineering projects, and do field work to protect and improve the status of rare creatures. Conservation issues include reed-bed and tree replanting, the protection of wild flowers and wading birds, and the preservation of wind and water mills.

Jobs with the NRA are advertised at local level, or in the *Guardian* and other publications. Graduate entrants to conservation posts, with degrees in biological or chemical science, are trained through work experience and supported in continuing education and studies for membership of professional institutes, including the Institution of Water and Environmental Management, the Royal Society of Chemistry and the Institute of Biology.

The environment protection section of the DoE employs a wide range of professional officers, many working in integrated teams with administrators. Together they develop and implement government policy towards protection of the environment including the supervision of a substantial research programme. The DoE represents the UK during discussion of most aspects of pollution control in international forums, notably in the European Community.

The Property Services Agency

The PSA is the largest design and construction organisation in the UK, with an annual budget of around £10 billion. It has a strong interest in the conservation of old buildings, as well as new, and has been involved in restoring the Palm House at Kew Gardens and advising on the new British Library in London.

The Department of Energy

The Department of Energy was set up in its present form in 1974. It is responsible for the development of national energy policy, including the management of current sources of energy and development of new sources, energy efficiency, representing the government in dealings with the nationalised energy industries (coal and electricity) and the United Kingdom Atomic Energy Authority, sponsoring the oil and nuclear power construction industries, overseeing government interest in the development of offshore oil and gas, and dealing with international energy affairs.

The Department employs about 1,150 people, of whom all but about 170 work at departmental headquarters in London. The work of the department is divided into different sectors, of which the following relate to conservation.

Energy Efficiency Office. This is the division with general responsibility for the government's energy efficiency policy. Activities include an educational programme aimed at furthering conservation, the promotion of efficiency measures, research into and development of new measures, and technical advice to industry, commerce, the construction industry, local authorities and other large energy consumers.

Energy and international policy. This division is responsible for the government's energy policy and for UK policy on international energy affairs. Activities include the environmental aspects of energy policy, relations with the European Community and other countries on energy policy, and energy pricing.

Energy Technology Support Unit. This sector consists of 40 professional staff of scientists and technical advisers who operate research, development and demonstration programmes dedicated to energy efficiency.

Information. This is the division responsible for the Department's public relations, press liaison, publicity and publications.

Other specialist divisions are assigned to work on nuclear energy, coal, electricity, gas, oil, and petroleum policy. They manage government input into these areas, review supply and demand, and carry out research into public safety.

Overseas Development Administration (ODA)

The ODA is part of the Foreign and Commonwealth Office, and formulates and carries out British development aid policy, much of which is directed at Third World countries.

Aid is in the form of financial and technical co-operation to help developing countries with specific projects (such as building roads, setting up fisheries, forestry research or emergency relief) and with long-term programmes (such as forest management, soil conservation, or energy development). A large amount of aid goes into conservation and resource management projects.

The ODA runs specialist departments dealing with projects in rural development, natural resources, science, technology, health and population, education, and manpower. It finances a number of specialist research and advisory organisations, and has its own scientific unit, the Overseas Development Natural Resources Institute.

Natural Resources Institute. This is the ODA's in-house scientific unit at Chatham in Kent, comprising some 500 scientific and support staff.

The Institute's mandate is to promote sustainable development of renewable natural resources in the tropics.

The main areas of work are: resource assessment and farming systems; integrated pest management; and food science and crop utilisation. The Institute has purpose-built laboratories and a world-class library, and the work covers applied research, surveys, the transfer of technology and programmes of advice and consultancy. The staff collaborate in scientific projects at home and overseas, and most travel overseas on short- and long-term assignments, to around 60 countries across the developing world. The main disciplines are chemistry, biochemistry, land use, livestock nutrition, food technology, engineering and economics.

Other ODA activities include research into water management and conservation, re-afforestation and forest management, and the development of energy and fishery resources.

The Natural Environment Research Council (NERC)

The NERC is one of the government's five Research Councils, and was set up in 1965 to research physical and biological sciences relating to the natural environment. With more than 2,500 staff, it is one of the largest employers of school leavers and graduates with qualifications and an interest in the life sciences.

Like the other Research Councils, the NERC is autonomous and operates under a Royal Charter. It is funded by the Department of Education and Science and carries out its research through a series of specialist institutes, and gives grants and awards for research in universities and other institutes of higher education. It also advises government and industry on environmental matters.

The NERC has 21 institutes, of which the following are of particular interest to environmental scientists.

The Institute of Terrestrial Ecology studies the ecology of land ecosystems, including changes in land use, the effects of pollutants, and threats posed to endangered species. It employs 249 staff.

The Unit of Comparative Plant Ecology studies the interaction of plants with their environment, and the mechanisms controlling plant distribution and vegetation structure. It employs 15 staff.

The Institute of Virology and Environmental Microbiology studies viruses, virus diseases of insects, and their effects on other forms of life. It employs 68 staff.

The Institute of Freshwater Ecology studies the ecological characteristics of inland waters and the ways in which water is used. It employs 100 staff.

The Institute of Hydrology studies the phases of the hydrological cycle and the problems of managing and using water as a natural resource. It employs 161 staff.

The British Geological Survey undertakes geological research to provide information for the exploration and use of mineral, water and energy resources. It employs 795 staff.

The Institute of Oceanographic Sciences Deacon Laboratory studies the characteristics of the ocean, oceanic resources, and the structure and topography of the ocean bed. It employs 162 staff.

The Plymouth Marine Laboratory carries out inter-disciplinary research into estuarine, coastal, shelf and oceanic ecosystems. It employs 149 staff.

The Dunstaffnage Marine Laboratory undertakes a variety of marine surveys, including environmental impact assessments and environmental management and monitoring. It employs 47 staff.

The Proudman Oceanographic Laboratory studies the theory, observation and numerical modelling of sea levels worldwide, shelf and slope processes and circulation. It employs 80 staff.

The Sea Mammal Research Unit studies the role of seals and whales in marine ecosystems and the effects of management policies on their populations. It employs 16 staff.

The British Antarctic Survey undertakes year-round research in the Antarctic into topics such as terrestrial, freshwater and marine ecology, and helps to formulate policy on the rational management of the Antarctic environment. It employs 414 staff.

Recruitment of staff is handled either directly by the Council, or by the Civil Service Commission, depending upon the grade of the vacancy.

Scientific staff make up the bulk of NERC employees, and vacancies are normally advertised in the national press, scientific journals, and universities. The most junior level is the *assistant scientific officer*, who needs four GCSEs or equivalent, including English language, a science or maths subject, and not more than one of an artistic, commercial or domestic nature. Promotion is to *scientific officer*, for which post candidates need to be aged under 27, and have a degree in a science, maths or engineering subject, degree standard membership of a professional institution, or a Higher BTEC Certificate in a science, maths or engineering subject, or equivalent.

Candidates for the post of *higher scientific officer* should have the same qualifications as a scientific officer, in addition to which they need at least two years' postgraduate research or development experience (if they have a first or second class honours degree or equivalent), or else at least five years' appropriate experience. They should normally be aged under 30. The most senior scientific post is that of *senior scientific officer*, for which candidates should be aged between 25 and 32, should have a first or second class degree in a science, maths or engineering subject, or equivalent, and at least four years' postgraduate or other approved experience.

Administrative staff are employed to support the scientific staff with clerical and executive duties. Candidates for the post of *administrative officer* should have five GCSEs or equivalent, including English, and should be aged over 17½. For *executive officer* posts, candidates should have two A levels or equivalent, passed at the same sitting, in addition to three GCSEs, and should be aged over 17½.

The Ministry of Agriculture, Fisheries and Food (MAFF)
As its name implies, MAFF is responsible for carrying out government policy on agriculture, fisheries and food.

Within that wide spectrum MAFF's concerns include:

▫ monitoring animal health and welfare;

- implementing environmental protection schemes;
- maintaining public health standards in the manufacture, preparation and distribution of foods;
- conserving the marine and fresh water environments.

Given that more than 70 per cent of our total land surface is farmed, and that fishing is one of our principal offshore industries, the degree of MAFF's influence over the natural environment is considerable.

MAFF seeks, in drawing up policies for agriculture, to achieve a reasonable balance between the interests of agriculture, the social and economic needs of rural areas, the conservation of the countryside and the promotion of its enjoyment by the public. Conservation interests are consulted when new policies are being formulated and a number of measures of direct benefit to countryside conservation have been introduced in recent years, including the effects of pesticides on wildlife. MAFF employs about 10,000 staff, of whom about half are specialists in scientific or technical areas. About a third of the staff work at the London headquarters, and the remainder are at MAFF's five regional offices and in Wales.

Most of the openings for environmental scientists and planners are with the Agricultural Development and Advisory Service (ADAS), a department of MAFF which provides technical information and advice to farmers. Much of the work involves integrated environmental considerations with agriculture and the rural economy. ADAS provides free advice on conservation matters to farmers.

Another department of MAFF which is of interest is the Directorate of Fisheries Research, based at Lowestoft, which researches the commercial exploitation of fish and shellfish stocks, and marine and freshwater pollution. There are openings for marine ecologists, biologists and fish biologists, biochemists, geneticists, chemists, physicists and geologists, and experts in fish disease, population dynamics and operational research.

The Forestry Commission
Since it was founded in 1919, the Forestry Commission has been the government body responsible for the nation's forests. It owns just under half of Britain's 2 million hectares of productive forest, and is responsible for promoting the interests of forestry, for the efficient production of wood for industry, for the development of afforestation, and for the welfare and conservation of wildlife in the forests. Many areas within the Commission's woodlands have been designated Sites of Special Scientific Interest and National Nature Reserves, and a few have been set up as Forest Nature Reserves. The overall policy is to balance the needs of wildlife with those of the timber industry.

Openings within the Forestry Commission are different from those in the private forestry sector (see Chapter 4). The Commission divides the country into seven conservancies, each headed by a *conservator of forests*. The conservator is helped by a team of senior managers with responsibility for general forest management, harvesting and marketing, conservation and estate work.

Each conservancy is in turn divided into districts, usually containing several forests of more than 4,000 hectares each, which are run by forest district offices. These are responsible for running the Commission's own planting, harvesting and marketing operations and maintaining the wildlife and environmental aspects of the district.

Forestry jobs are at three levels: forest worker, forest officer IV and forest officer II. There are occasional vacancies for wildlife rangers who look after the forest environment.

Forest worker. Anyone who is physically fit and interested in manual work outdoors can apply for work as a forest worker. The work is mainly manual or operating machines in the forest with a wide range of work including fencing, planting, draining, weeding, pruning, timber harvesting and nursery work. Training is given to enable forest workers to qualify as forest craftsmen and for further advancement to ranger and foreman or to wildlife ranger. Jobs are advertised locally.

Forest officer IV. Forest officers at this level must possess a BTEC National Diploma in Forestry *or* a SCOTVEC National Certificate appropriate to management-level modules in forestry *or* a degree in forestry *or* a corporate membership of the Institute of Chartered Foresters *or* a City and Guilds Phase IV Certificate in Forestry.

Officers on this grade are technical supervisors with responsibility for planning and controlling operations (harvesting etc) and for the protection of forest property. They also maintain good relations with neighbouring landowners, organisations and individuals who wish to use the forest for sport or recreation. Experienced officers are also employed on specialist duties such as training, work study, wildlife conservation and research.

Forest officer II. Candidates must possess an honours degree in forestry or in a closely related subject with substantial forestry content *or* a postgraduate degree in forestry *or* an equivalent higher qualification *or* a corporate membership of the Institute of Chartered Foresters. Candidates must also hold a driving licence.

Officers in this grade perform a variety of junior management functions mainly in helping to plan and control the Commission's policies and operations. There are opportunities to undertake more specialised work such as recreation, training or research. Most forest officers will be in regular contact with the general public and the professions.

Wildlife ranger. Formal qualifications are not required but relevant previous experience is essential. All wildlife rangers are thoroughly trained.

The work entails protecting and conserving the forest environment, controlling pests and protecting forest wildlife, as well as creating and maintaining suitable habitats. Rangers also guide and assist the public who visit the forests and enforce the by-laws. A 24-hour commitment to the job is necessary.

The Forestry Commission also has administrative assistants, administrative officers and executive officers in its headquarters and offices, and there are openings for scientists, mechanical and civil engineers, land agents and clerks of works.

Career prospects. Forestry is primarily concerned with growing trees for commercial exploitation, and as such requires an understanding of the needs and structure of the forest environment. Without conservation, exploitation could not be sustained. Competition for entry to forestry is high at all levels.

Case Study
Ben is a forest worker with the Forestry Commission. He left school when he was 16 and did a variety of odd jobs before applying for his current job, which he has been doing for just over two years. He was attracted to it originally because it meant working out of doors, but now he sees it as a career.

> I'm still on the first rung of the ladder, but I am hoping to stay with the Commission and work my way up. At least this way you pick up working experience as you go along. It's mostly very hard work and it can get a bit boring at times, but there is something exciting about working in forests. I'm part of a team working under a foreman, and we do a whole variety of jobs. Just before the planting season you could be doing fencing and maintenance work, then you get down to planting transplants during the early spring. The summer is taken up with weeding and clearing the new plantations, and then the thinning begins in the autumn. In between I've been sent off on short courses on how to use and maintain machinery and forest management. I would like to keep on working out of doors all my life, so I want to avoid being promoted to a desk job within the Commission. I've got my eyes on a job as a warden eventually.

Chapter 6

Working for Statutory Bodies

Introduction

Much of the responsibility for managing wildlife and natural resources in the UK lies with statutory bodies – that is, bodies set up under law. They lie somewhere between the voluntary and government sectors, being funded largely by the government but not actual government bodies.

The main bodies entrusted with conservation and the environment are the three new country conservation bodies which have taken over from the former Nature Conservancy Council that covered the whole of the UK. They are English Nature, the Nature Conservancy Council for England, Scottish Natural Heritage (formed by a merging of the Nature Conservancy Council for Scotland and the Countryside Commission for Scotland), and the Countryside Council for Wales; plus the Countryside Commission, 11 national park authorities, and the Forestry Commission which is a full government department (see Chapter 5). Between them they offer a range of openings for administrators, planners and scientists.

English Nature

English Nature advises the government on nature conservation in England, and promotes, directly and through others, the conservation of England's wildlife and natural features within the wider setting of the UK and its international responsibilities. It is based at Peterborough, at the headquarters of the former Nature Conservancy Council, and its work continues to be to select, establish and manage national nature reserves, and to identify and notify the Sites of Special Scientific Interest. There are currently over 140 nature reserves and 3,500 SSSIs. The Council provides advice and information about nature conservation and support, and conducts relevant research. The Council is also consulted by local authorities about industrial processes in England that involve discharges to the land, air or water, if the authorities are asked to authorise operations that may affect local SSSIs.

English Nature works with the Nature Conservancy Council for Scotland and the Countryside Council for Wales on UK and international conservation issues through the Joint Nature Conservation Committee. (The Department of the Environment for Northern Ireland has parallel responsibilities.)

Although it is not a government department, English Nature offers the same rates of pay, conditions of service and recruitment regulations as the Civil Service, and demands certain minimum qualifications or experience.

English Nature has increased its staff, compared with the former NCC posts in England, with 724 permanent staff of 338 administrators, 239 science grades (the greatest increase) and 147 field, professional and technical grades. The Council intends to increase staffing support for the regional offices. Other aims are to:

- Implement the Earth Science Conservation Strategy, with publications, lectures and public meetings to encourage owners, users and managers of earth science sites to become involved in their conservation; briefs for earth SSSIs and a programme of integrated earth science (everything to do with the formation and surface of the earth) and wildlife conservation management of coastlines.
- Begin new reserve management projects to protect SSSIs that are in danger of deteriorating.
- Pilot a species recovery programme.

Openings
Scientific staff. Openings here are mainly for graduates, and the usual point of entry is the *assistant conservation officer (ACO)*. The ACO is the Council's public face, and is responsible to the *conservation officer* for a variety of duties. ACOs spend most of their time identifying habitats with high nature conservation interest. This involves surveying and assessing scientific sites, working with the owners on the conservation of statutory sites, working with local planning authorities on any developments that affect wildlife and nature, consulting voluntary conservation bodies, and conservation education.

Good first degrees in biology, botany, zoology, geology or geography are usually the minimum requirement for ACOs, and an MSc in conservation/ecology would strengthen your application. Previous experience is usually the deciding factor, so any voluntary work undertaken with clubs, societies, charities or natural history groups would be useful. Most ACOs are classed as *higher scientific officers* (applicants must have had at least two years' relevant postgraduate experience), or *scientific officers*.

Vacancies are advertised in national papers and journals, and competition is usually stiff. The Council is prepared to keep details of applicants on file for ACO posts for a period of 12 months, and to notify them when suitable vacancies come up.

Reserve staff. If competition for scientific staff vacancies is stiff, then competition for posts as site managers for the reserves is fierce. There are more than 140 National Nature Reserves, and the Council needs wardens to oversee their management, which includes everything from supervising voluntary wardens and estate staff to patrolling the reserve, carrying out maintenance, advising and guiding visitors, conserving wildlife, carrying out scientific recording and monitoring, maintaining records and reports, servicing scientific research work, maintaining nature trails, and liaising with neighbouring landowners.

Posts for wardens are usually advertised in the spring. Applicants must be over 26, good all-round naturalists, able to undertake basic scientific survey work, have a full current driving licence and be able to maintain vehicles. They should also have estate work and forestry skills, and be able to face the public with confidence. Formal educational qualifications are not compulsory, but A levels or a degree in a life science certainly help.

The work of a warden is hard and demanding, and calls for long hours out of doors in all weathers. The Council also has openings for unpaid voluntary wardens to work in evenings and at weekends, and experience picked up in this way is usually the best stepping-stone to a full-time post.

Executive and clerical staff. Recruitment to executive grades is carried out by the Civil Service Commission as part of their normal programme for jobs in government service, details of which are given in Chapter 5. Clerical openings also follow normal Civil Service procedures, but recruitment is managed directly by English Nature. The work includes accounting, library services, establishments, registry, land agency work, servicing committees and general administration.

Estate workers work in manual jobs in reserve management, carrying out hedging, ditching, felling, reed-cutting, clearing and other tasks. They pick up sound practical conservation knowledge which stands them in good stead if they want to become reserve wardens. The few vacancies that arise are advertised locally by English Nature's regional offices.

Career Prospects

English Nature provides satisfying openings for conservationists, provided they have the initial experience and qualifications to be offered a job. Once in the Council, they can compete for higher level posts and work their way up the organisation, and prospects for career advancement are good. Entering at a higher level demands correspondingly higher qualifications.

Scottish Natural Heritage

Scottish Natural Heritage is a merging of the Nature Conservancy Council for Scotland with the Countryside Commission for Scotland, on April 1, 1992. The responsibility of Scottish Natural Heritage includes 'the flora and fauna of Scotland, its geological and physiographical features, its natural beauty and amenity'. The work is similar to the work of English Nature, including managing National Nature Reserves and Marine Nature Reserves, selecting SSSIs, conservation of protected plant and animal species, research, and raising awareness about nature conservation. SNH projects include the conservation of an endangered species of plant or animal, special habitats, helping schools create wildlife gardens in their grounds and the regeneration of native woodland.

Between them the two groups forming SNH have a staff of over 460; their skills cover ecology, geography, geology, biology, communications, education, landscape architecture, planning, land use management, archaeology, graphics and cartographics, and many other fields.

The main types of employment are similar to English Nature and the old Nature Conservancy Council, with Assistant Regional Officers, Scientist Officers, Earth Science Division, Field Survey Units and Specialist Development Officers, Reserve Wardens and Estate Workers, plus executive and administrative staff.

Countryside Council for Wales

The Countryside Council for Wales is the organisation that deals with countryside matters in Wales on behalf of the government. It provides advice on countryside matters to ministers and government departments as well as enabling others, including local authorities, voluntary organisations and interested individuals, to pursue countryside management projects through grant aid.

The Council advises the government and local authorities on matters that affect SSSIs, National Parks, Areas of Outstanding Natural Beauty (AONB), and on relevant Environmental Impact Assessments. The council also advises and comments in response to consultation on development plans and local planning applications, and takes part in public consultation exercises at national and local levels. The council would also respond to EC directives that affect its development in Wales through the joint Nature Conservation Committee, in conjunction with the related bodies in England and Scotland. The advice given by the Council is based on the experience of conservation bodies, ecologists and countryside managers, gained since the 1949 Countryside Act.

Advice is offered to owners and occupiers of rural land, voluntary organisations committed to the care of the countryside and the water companies.

The Council employs over 200 staff throughout Wales, including scientists, rangers and wardens, and also uses expertise provided by specialist organisations.

Wales has three National Parks, 47 National Nature Reserves, five AOBBs and about 800 SSSIs.

The Council is responsible for conserving the natural features and wildlife of Wales and the intrinsic quality of the landscape. It also promotes opportunity for access to the countryside.

The Countryside Commission

The Countryside Commission replaced the National Parks Commission in 1968, and was charged with responsibility for the conservation and enhancement of the countryside and promoting access and the provision of recreational facilities. Then part of the Civil Service, it now has greater independence and manages its own recruitment for posts. There is one

Commission for England. Those for Wales and Scotland are merged into new country conservancy bodies.

The Commission's responsibilities include designating and supporting (with grants and advice) national parks, areas of outstanding natural beauty, national trails and bridleways. It also has a research and experimental programme and provides publicity and information about the work it is doing. On a national level it gives advice to government on countryside policy generally, and on a local level to conservation bodies and local authorities.

Openings

The Commission employs about 200 staff, half of whom are employed in the head office at Cheltenham and the other half in the network of eight regional offices. There are three divisions:

1. **Resources**, which is responsible for the provision of support services including programme planning, finance, personnel and office services.

2. **Regional**, which consists of head office staff and seven regional offices and the office for Wales employing between four and seven staff in each office, to promote the Commission's policies regionally, work with local authorities and individuals, and manage grants for countryside work.

3. **Policy**, which consists of five branches which advise on and develop policy in their particular subject areas.

Conservation. Landscape conservation, monitoring of land-use trends, including agricultural policies, forestry and woodland management (multi-purpose forestry), water and land drainage. The branch employs suitably qualified life scientists, planners, landscape architects and economists.

Recreation and access. Country parks, national trails and bridleways, rights of way and access, commons, 'enjoying the countryside', management of countryside for people. It also advises on information and visitor services.

National parks and planning. National parks, areas of outstanding natural beauty and heritage coasts. It also covers development control and planning issues.

Training and voluntary action. Countryside staff training, community action, voluntary bodies, voluntary and paid work in the countryside. The branch provides policy direction on voluntary body issues and employment and training in the countryside.

Communications. Press relations, publications, general advice to the public and the library.

Career Prospects

Because of its small size, the Countryside Commission offers few openings, and because it owns no land it does not employ part-time staff in the same way as the other two statutory bodies. As a result of restructuring, it is likely to expand its field of activities. For the time being it offers planners, scientists, and national and regional administrators the chance to be involved closely with national conservation activities. Recruitment is handled nationally.

The National Parks

Although the Countryside Commission is responsible for the general management and welfare of national parks, each is controlled by its own board or committee. There are 11 national parks in England and Wales (Scotland has none), of which two (the Peak and the Lake District) have their own park boards. Dartmoor, Northumberland, the Pembrokeshire Coast, Snowdonia, Brecon Beacons, Exmoor, the North York Moors and the Yorkshire Dales are run by county committees and the Broads Authority, which has similar status to a National Park Authority, is responsible for the Broads.

Openings

Each board is autonomous and is responsible for planning, buying land, administration, recruiting staff, and determining salary grades of employees. So it is difficult to generalise about opportunities, although all the parks tend to employ common grades of staff to carry out broadly similar duties.

The annual budget of each board varies considerably. This is reflected in the number of staff employed: the Peak is the largest employer, with over 150 full-time staff and 200 part-time and seasonal staff, and Northumberland the smallest, with approximately 30 in four main grades of service.

Management, administration and planning. This area consists largely of senior or professional staff charged with the management of the parks, who are responsible for liaising with the owners of public and private land that falls within the borders of each park. They resolve the different demands of development and conservation, manage budgets, buy new land, and plan and provide guidelines for the management of the parks. There are openings for professional planners, surveyors, park and recreation administrators, and other executive and clerical staff. About 40 per cent of national park staff are employed in this sector.

Information. Because national parks exist for the enjoyment of the thousands of visitors who visit them annually, the provision of visitor centres and information facilities is a major function. Staff with a background in information and education are employed to run the centres and to work directly with the public. Duties include setting up displays, publishing leaflets and guides, working as sales assistants, running educational facilities, and providing general guidance.

Wardening. The daily management and upkeep of the parks is in the hands of wardens and rangers, who are responsible for guiding visitors, carrying out conservation policy, protecting wildlife, supervising management work, helping with information and interpretation, and keeping in touch with local landowners. The qualifications necessary are similar to those for Conservancy Council wardens: a high degree of experience, relevant skills and abilities and a deep interest in natural history and conservation.

Project and estate management. Carrying out estate projects is the job of a combined team of professional estate managers and manual workers. They maintain recreational and visitor facilities, look after roads, paths and nature trails, carry out general maintenance of the parks, operate machinery, and undertake other tasks.

The parks have openings for scientists, planners, administrators, and executive, clerical and manual staff, and some employ ecologists, naturalists, foresters, soil scientists and other conservation specialists.

They also employ a substantial number of part-time and seasonal staff, mostly during the summer season when the number of visitors increases sharply. Many of these staff are students working in their vacations, school leavers, and members of government job-creation schemes. They are employed as information assistants, weekend wardens, seasonal rangers, student researchers, car-park attendants and services staff. Vacancies are normally open to existing staff before being advertised publicly.

Career Prospects

The level of opportunity varies with the economic climate and the budget policies of local authorities. Despite the fact that salary levels are generally below par, competition for vacancies is always keen, so candidates need a high degree of ability and experience. Working in one of the national parks means being involved in a central area of national conservation activity.

Case Study

George has been working as a national nature reserve warden for the past five years. He was born and brought up only five miles from the reserve, so he knows the area intimately.

> It was the reserve that first got me interested in natural history and conservation, when my uncle used to bring me along to bird-watch when I was at school. He knew everyone who worked here, and it was only a matter of time before I was working here at weekends and helping out with the information centre. After leaving school I took an environmental studies course at college, but even though I saw it through I am not sure it helped to prepare me for the practicalities of working on a reserve. You learn mostly through experience, and from being taught by the older hands. My experience as a voluntary warden was what really got me this job – I heard that there were 250 applicants.
>
> I love the work. The pay is poor and we sometimes feel a bit forgotten by head office, but I'm really my own man and it is up to us to make sure that everything is run properly, that good facilities for visitors are maintained, and that people

get the most out of coming here. You also feel a strong responsibility for the welfare of the wildlife. The job involves a lot of research and surveying, as well as routine reserve maintenance. It's hard work, with long hours out of doors in rain and shine, but time doesn't matter because it's more a way of life than a job.

Chapter 7

Education and Research

Introduction

Conservation sprang from concern about the degradation of the natural environment. It was the visible effects of that degradation – pollution, the loss of forests, the destruction of wildlife etc – that moved people to act, rather than an accumulation of data from which science was able to identify negative trends. Early conservationists tended to 'patch up' problems wherever they surfaced rather than look for the underlying causes.

Part of the problem lay in the fact that they knew (and we still know) little about the structure of the natural environment and about the threats it faced and faces. The knowledge we now have has been accumulated in a short space of time, and we have probably learned as much in the past 20 years as we learned in the preceding two centuries. There has been an increased emphasis given to both environmental education and research in conservation in recent years.

Environmental Education

Education is now widely regarded as being one of the most important environmental priorities, but much of the initiative for its development still rests with the voluntary sector. Environmental studies is still a rare option in British secondary schools, and ecology is barely taught at all. Geography, biology, botany and zoology are, on the other hand, widely taught, and occasionally give rise to more specialised fields of environmental study.

The options are much wider in higher education, where conservation, ecology and environmental studies are more frequently offered alongside the life sciences and professional training in planning, forestry, estate management and related topics. Outside the education establishment, a number of voluntary bodies are developing increasingly thoughtful education programmes.

Teaching in Schools
The teaching profession is a career option that offers a number of openings for environmentalists. The number of schools offering environmental studies and science as GCSE and A-level options is growing, and

a number of organisations (notably the Council for Environmental Education and the National Association for Environmental Education) both promote environmental teaching in schools and offer students and teachers guidance and assistance.

Teachers who run classes in almost any subject can often touch on environmental matters within the normal curriculum. Alternatively, a teacher who expresses an interest in teaching environmental studies may well get a sympathetic hearing from the school authorities, so it may be up to the teacher to take the initiative.

Training is via a course leading to a degree and qualified teacher status (QTS) or PGCE. Entrants to teaching are normally graduates and need a minimum of five GCSEs, including English language and mathematics, and an additional two A levels would be useful, especially in environmental studies or science. Entrants to universities generally need five GCSEs and two A levels, and following graduation they would study for a one-year Postgraduate Certificate of Education (PGCE).

Teaching in Higher Education

As well as offering courses in every branch of life science, many universities and colleges run professional courses in resource management, planning and conservation, and specialist courses in subjects such as plant ecology, pollution control, the management of genetic resources and alternative sources of energy.

Nearly all these institutions are currently suffering from spending cuts, so there is little new building. New departments are not being opened, and there are few vacancies. Jobs are therefore at a premium and even a high level of experience and academic achievement does not guarantee employment.

For those who are able to find jobs, entry is almost always through postgraduate research and study. Many university tutors and lecturers combine teaching with research and administration, so research interests and abilities are essential. Former polytechnics, now with university status, are not as much involved in environmental research at present.

Most institutions of further education are run by local authorities. They may either specialise in vocational training or offer a more general range of education. They vary considerably in size and in the scope of their courses. Part-time and evening classes in specialist minority subjects offer scope for the environmental teacher.

The minimum qualifications for university teaching vary. Someone with a firm background in research and a high level of academic achievement is likely to be favoured, but this is by no means certain. The demands are similar for polytechnic teaching posts but working experience is also useful, especially if it is in a field related to the teaching post. Someone wanting to teach environmental studies, for example, would probably need a few years' experience in resource planning and management or conservation.

Conservation Education

Many environmental and conservation groups, both voluntary and statutory, run national and local education programmes that employ qualified teachers and youth group leaders. Some programmes are designed largely to promote the aims of individual bodies by involving young people in conservation and the appreciation of natural history, while others have more general aims. Many young people take part by virtue of their membership of the body, while others take part in projects run by different bodies in their areas of interest.

So, for example, a charity might run a schools lecture programme, a natural history society might take parties of schoolchildren around a local nature reserve, an ornithological group may involve children in bird-watching and surveying, and a practical conservation group may run projects for young people at weekends and in school holidays.

Most of the larger conservation bodies have been running youth membership schemes for many years. They were mainly limited to subscription schemes, with children paying their dues and receiving magazines and other material in return. The current trend is towards programmes that involve children actively in conservation, coupled with efforts to encourage schools to include environmental studies in their curricula.

Voluntary organisations employ education officers and youth group leaders to run these programmes. Teaching experience is desirable, but by no means essential; a proven ability to run teaching projects and an interest in working with children and schools are the minimum requirements. Much greater emphasis is being given to carefully structured education programmes.

Other Fields

There are also openings in adult and continuing education, with local education authorities and private field centres, and with a few correspondence colleges. The adult and extra-mural education field offers short part-time courses that cater for all interests. Teaching is conducted mostly by part-time staff, and most posts go to people with part-time teaching experience. There is considerable potential for anyone interested in teaching specialist environmental courses on a part-time basis.

The Field Studies Council

The Field Studies Council, founded in 1943, is an independent charity that runs 10 field centres in England and Wales. These hold short residential courses in environmental studies, ecology, biology, geography and geology.

The Council runs courses for teachers to help them teach environmental studies in their own schools. There are courses in project and field work, analysis techniques, teaching ecology, geography and GCSE field work. The Council also employs graduates in full-time teaching posts and non-graduates in temporary summer work. Competition for the few full-time posts is very keen. Each Centre is run by a warden, assisted by two, three or four tutors, who may be helped by research assistants and/or conservation officers, plus administrative and domestic staff. Minimum qualifications for an academic post are an honours degree in an appropriate subject, and a teaching qualification is an advantage. The courses are run between mid February and early November for sixth-form, GCSE and younger pupils and for teachers, university students, professional people and adult amateur naturalists. This leaves the winter months largely free for research and course preparation.

Case Studies

Anne runs a youth education programme in Wales for a national environmental group.

> I have wanted to work in conservation as long as I can remember. From about the age of five I was a member of just about every junior wildlife watchers group that was going, and I took part in a lot of projects while I was at school. I took A levels in zoology and botany and then read zoology at university. It was while I was there that I began to realise that getting my ideal job in conservation wouldn't be as easy as I had thought. Graduates from two or three years before my year all seemed to be working in anything but zoology.
>
> About six months before I graduated I started applying for likely jobs, but had had no luck by the time I graduated. I was determined not to go on the dole, so I enrolled for a postgraduate certificate of education. I applied for jobs continuously for a year - even ones that were only vaguely related to conservation. Altogether I went through 56 applications from which I got 14 interviews but no jobs. My 57th application was for a secretarial job in the membership department of a conservation group, and I was accepted. Just by luck, the offer of the job I'm now in came up. It's working for the same organisation, and I think it was because they knew where my real interests lay that I was given preference over outside applicants.
>
> The job is everything I want for the time being. I was given virtual *carte blanche* to set the scheme up, and I'm now worked off my feet arranging field trips, writing and designing information packs, commissioning posters, producing audio-visual programmes, and starting up school groups. I'm the first to realise how lucky I have been to get this job - it was certainly worth the wait.

Bernard is a postgraduate student who supports himself by giving evening classes at a college of further education.

> I was fortunate enough to have a superb biology teacher at school who gave me my interest in natural history. She encouraged me to go on and read environmental studies at college with the idea of going on to teach. I got my first teaching post in an unusual place: holding classes on conservation for commuters on the train to college in my final year. I had to commute 90 minutes each way, and groups of commuters were getting together to hold classes to relieve the boredom. One day a college lecturer joined the group; we got talking, and he recommended that I approach a few colleges of further education and ask about part-time posts. I applied to three or four colleges and was lucky enough to get my present post, which I am now using to support me while I read for a master's degree, something which I didn't think I would be able to do for years.
>
> The job is mostly quite good fun, because I have a rapport with the students, who are nearly all older than me and don't mind getting into a few arguments and debates. Occasionally I have to take small classes of passive students, and

I also get a bit frustrated by the irregularity of attendance. On the whole, though, I'm getting good teaching experience.

Research Opportunities

Research is a process of inquiry, scientific study and critical investigation – the collection, analysis and interpretation of facts. Because knowledge is not an absolute quantity – we can never know everything there is to know about something – there will always be scope for research. As far as our understanding of the natural environment is concerned, we are only just beginning to collect the facts. The active study of ecology is less than 100 years old, and we still do not fully understand the mechanisms of the biosphere. There are almost limitless opportunities to pioneer new avenues of study. The only constraints are financial. Perhaps because research is less obviously productive than teaching or applied fieldwork, it often suffers in the wake of spending cuts. And yet without research, knowledge suffers.

There are research opportunities in four main areas.

The Private Sector

Voluntary bodies, non-governmental organisations, and research institutes are responsible for the bulk of existing research programmes.

Charities either carry out their own research or support independent research with grants. Most of this support goes to universities, research institutes, and individuals with a reputation in research. However, almost anyone who can draw up a useful project proposal, give some proof of their own suitability, enlist the support of referees, and convince a charity that the project deserves support will be eligible for assistance.

There are several private research institutes carrying out research into population issues, Third World development, resource management, and the life sciences. They employ staff in a variety of capacities: visiting fellows, senior researchers, scientific officers and research assistants. Normal requirements are a first degree or equivalent qualification, combined with research experience and proven aptitude. The institutes work extensively with universities and the government, and maintain high standards of academic research and achievement.

Academic Research

The amount of research undertaken by universities and other centres of higher education that offer courses in environmental conservation and management is comparable to that of the private sector. Faculties, departments and affiliated research units generally devote more time to research and investigation than to teaching, and make considerable contributions to both general environmental knowledge and to specialised fields of study. As with teaching, finding a job in academic research demands a high level of experience and proven research ability, generally coupled with the possession of a higher degree and published work. Every aspect of conservation, resource management and the life sciences is scrutinised and studied.

Government Research

The government employs about 500 research officers to study the impact and implications of government policy and to help determine future needs. Many work for the Resource and Planning Research Group (RPRG), which studies policy on resource management and the environment, and some work on planning policy in the Department of the Environment.

In the Ministry of Agriculture, Fisheries and Food most scientific research work is carried on at the ADAS Central Sciences Laboratories at Slough, Tolworth (where a group studies the effect of pesticides on wildlife), Worplesdon and Harpenden; research into fish cultivation and the effects of pollution on the aquatic environment is carried out in the Directorate of Fisheries Research laboratories at Lowestoft, Burnham-on-Crouch (non-radioactive marine pollution), Conwy and Weymouth. There is also some research into pollution at MAFF's Food Safety Directorate Torry Research Station at Aberdeen. Research officers are also employed in the Agricultural Scientific Services and Fisheries Research Services of the Scottish Office.

The Laboratory of the Government Chemist, the government's focal point for analytical science, has a programme supporting the protection of the environment, scientists analyse foodstuffs, agricultural materials, and toxic metals and other hazardous materials of environmental interest.

Those working for the Overseas Development Administration are at the Natural Resources Institute, providing information on the economics of plant and animal resources in developing countries. In the Ministry of Agriculture, Fisheries and Food, most researchers work for the Agricultural Development and Advisory Service on land use studies. Research officers are also employed in equivalent capacities in the Welsh Office and the Central Research Unit of the Scottish Office.

Most government research officers are qualified in geography, agricultural economics, economics, economic geography, or an equivalent area.

The Industrial Sector

People in commerce and industry are gradually taking more interest in the environmental impact of their activities, and they are supporting more research, either internally or by providing grants to research institutes. The number of scientists and planners employed in this work has grown over the past 20 years, but the field is still restricted. Few companies employ more than a handful of specialists, who will require a high level of experience and proven research ability. One of the largest employers of research scientists is ICI. The laboratories of ICI Agrochemicals Jealott's Hill Research Station, employing over 120, and Group Environmental Laboratory at Brixham are among several in the company studying environmental toxicology. Areas of research include discharges to rivers, lakes and the sea, problems of air pollution, the disposal of waste to land, and contamination of soil and groundwater. As with all areas of investigation into the natural environment, the industrial research sector is likely to expand.

Chapter 8

Opportunities for Scientists

Introduction

Science is the backbone of conservation, because without an understanding of the structure of the natural environment there can be no really coherent attempts to protect and maintain it; conservation has even been described as applied ecology. On that basis, it would seem logical that a training in life science would be the best of all possible backgrounds for a conservationist, and that it would almost guarantee a job. In fact, this is not so.

Amateur naturalists in the nineteenth century were largely responsible for the emergence of the notion of conserving habitat, but it was only when the work of biologists, botanists and zoologists revealed the interdependence of species and the complexity of the natural world that conservationists began to realise the importance of science.

Environmental management requires co-operation between people from several disciplines, social scientists and economists as well as biological and earth scientists. There are now a few degree courses combining these disciplines, as well as a larger number of postgraduate qualifications. For those wishing to enter the practical types of conservation work, rather than research and theoretical development, these broad degrees are a better preparation than those confined to one or two disciplines.

Biology

Biology is the study of life and its structure: the form, functions, anatomy, behaviour, origins, and distribution of the earth's plant and animal species. Because it cannot be studied in isolation from other life sciences, it demands broad scientific training. Biologists study the form and structure of living organisms, the characteristics of ecosystems, the effects of environmental change, and a host of related subjects.

Biologists tend to work in health services, local authorities, water companies, the National Rivers Authority, landscape design, environmental consultancy, agricultural and industrial research, food science, and medicine. Most large engineering and oil companies also employ biological ecologists as well as geologists. The Game Conservancy trains and employs biologists for management of game reserves, and biology is a useful discipline for land agents on large estates.

Botany

Botany is the science and study of the structure, form, function, distribution and classification of plants. It is one of the oldest life sciences, studied for centuries by amateur naturalists attracted by the proximity, beauty and abundance of plant life. Despite this heritage, it is only now coming into its own as an environmental science. Until about 10 to 15 years ago, plants came a very poor second to animals in the priorities of conservation. The realisation that no animal species can be protected in isolation from its natural habitat, the foundation of which is nearly always plant life, and that perhaps as many as 25,000 plant species are threatened with extinction, has finally brought botany and plant ecology to the forefront of conservation.

Zoology

Zoology is the study and science of the structure, functions, habits, distribution and classification of animal life. The zoologist studies the anatomy and physiology of species, their feeding, territorial and reproductive habits, population trends, the characteristics of their natural habitats, and the ways in which they interact with their environment.

There are some openings for zoologists in conservation.

Ecology

Ecology is the study of the relationship between plant and animal life and its natural environment. Because the web of life is so complex, relationships are many and varied. Ecologists study the impact of species on their habitat, population trends, the influence of climate on life, the food chain, reproduction, the structure of ecosystems, and the impact of human activity on nature.

Many life science degrees have a substantial ecological component, and several are primarily ecological.

Marine and Freshwater Biology

Marine and freshwater environments are the subject of a considerable proportion of biological research activity, so much so that marine and freshwater biology has become almost a science in its own right. The field covers the study of animal and plant life in rivers, lakes and the open sea, the management of water and fishery resources, the effects of pollution, and the characteristics of marine and freshwater ecosystems. Because it is a specialised field, the number of openings is restricted.

Oceanography

Oceanography is the study of the oceans: the pattern and fluctuations of currents, the distribution of marine animals and plants, water temperature and salinity (salt level), and the geophysical structure of the ocean floor.

Until recently the oceans have been thought of as a dumping ground, but more attention is now being paid to oceanic resources such as fisheries, offshore oil and minerals, with the result that oceanography, like marine biology, is assuming a more important role in the management of the marine environment.

Most oceanographers tend to be qualified in biology, zoology, physics or geology. There are very few courses in oceanography.

Biochemistry

Biochemistry is the study of the chemical and physical processes involved in the structure of animal and plant life, with emphasis on the form and functions of organisms. It makes a valuable contribution to the understanding of organic life, and may determine the basis of local ecosystem conservation. However, most biochemists opt for careers in research, education, medicine, and the agrochemical industry.

Soil Science

Soil is one of the most valuable of all natural resources. It supports not only agriculture but almost all terrestrial plant life as well. The conservation of soil has assumed new dimensions in recent decades as erosion, flooding, and the removal of plant cover have led to widespread losses of fertile soil cover.

Soil scientists classify and survey soil types, study soil microbiology and ecology, and experiment with different methods of soil management, weed control and crop production. Most soil scientists specialise after a general training in one or more of the main life sciences. There are openings in the UK (for example, with the Soil Survey of England and Wales), but the profession is more advanced in the United States. Specialists are also in demand in developing countries.

Maths and Chemistry

Maths is now essential for all management and consultancy work, as is the ability to use computer systems. Chemistry is necessary for most areas of work except for certain types of wardening.

Other Sciences

All life sciences are either combinations or extensions of three principal disciplines: biology, botany and zoology. Training in one of these opens up varied channels of specialisation in sciences such as microbiology (the study of micro-organisms), entomology (insects), ichthyology (fish), ornithology (birds), herpetology (reptiles), malacology (molluscs), and mycology (fungi), or more broadly based sciences such as bionomics (the study of the habits of living organisms in their natural environment) or genetics.

Qualifications

Anyone starting out on a career in environmental science has two options; to find work straight from school as a technician or laboratory assistant, usually taking qualifying examinations such as BTEC or RSA, or to go on to further education. The minimum requirements for school leavers wanting to start work right away are at least three GCSEs, including one in a relevant science. At least one additional A level would be an advantage.

Courses in life sciences are offered at universities, polytechnics, technical colleges and other centres of higher education throughout the country. General courses are available, and there are many first degrees on offer that specialise. Students must decide whether to take a general mixed discipline degree first, and then perhaps a more specific qualification later, or to specialise first and then take an 'applied' qualification. The normal requirements for entry to a course of higher education are five GCSEs (with at least one in a science subject) and two A levels in science subjects (one of which should relate closely to your chosen course). It is worth noting that sandwich courses offer opportunities for practical work experience and employers usually prefer applicants with such experience.

Openings

There may not be many openings for scientists with individual voluntary, statutory, government, or resource management organisations, but the number employed in all sectors makes conservation an important career option. The problem is that it is also a popular option, and the number of scientists who would like to work in conservation exceeds the number of vacancies.

The largest problem facing environmental scientists is that they are often compelled to compete for jobs that could be filled by candidates with a more general education, as a knowledge of science may be only one of several requirements. A second problem is that courses in ecology and environmental science offered at schools and centres of higher education are relatively new and untried, and are less familiar to employers. Third, many scientists are employed in research, a field susceptible to spending cuts.

On the other hand, there are advantages in having a science background. It can be an advantage, for example, when competing for vacancies in library and information work, writing and publishing, education, museum work, administration and planning.

For the candidate who succeeds in finding work in environmental science, the rewards are many and the openings varied. Research and development, ecology and field work, reserve management, the running of zoos and botanical gardens, and conservation policy are just some of the areas that need specialist knowledge.

Being Prepared
Understanding the profession, knowing where to look for jobs and anticipating demands can save a great deal of wasted time and energy. Because vacancies are rare you cannot afford to miss many opportunities through lack of preparation.

First, it is important not to specialise too early on in your career. A general education in one or more scientific disciplines will widen your options. Studying other sciences during training can be useful, and you can try to pick up part-time or unpaid practical experience and learn additional skills, such as computer science and data-handling techniques. Use holidays and weekends to go on field trips, undertake your own research projects, work as a voluntary warden, or take classes in related subjects.

Because practical experience is so important, it is advisable to work with local voluntary organisations in school and college holidays, and to become proficient in some aspect of conservation such as management of a particular habitat, identification of one or more groups of organisms, or organising teams of volunteers. Writing for local newsletters helps to develop a good reporting style and all these activities will get you in touch with other people in conservation. Almost all successful conservation scientists started out as amateurs with natural history or conservation as a hobby while they were still at school.

Second, be sure that you know the job market and all likely employers. Cast your net as widely as possible, and explore even remote possibilities. Join any professional societies linked with your science, attend their meetings, become active in their work, and meet as many other members as you can. One of them might point out a vacancy that you have not heard about, or might even be able to offer you part-time or full-time work.

Finally, start looking around and apply for jobs some time before you leave school, college, or university. Many organisations, with their eyes on school leavers or graduates coming on to the job market in the late summer, will start advertising jobs early in the year, in March or April. You should be prepared to compromise and to accept routine work as a lab assistant or technician if it arises. Such work will often give you the kind of useful experience that will help you to move on to something better. You may even be obliged to accept work for a while in a field unrelated to conservation, but with care you can turn such experience to your advantage.

Case Studies
Jane is a biologist with a government research department.

> When I decided to read biology at university I didn't really have any idea what I would do with it when I graduated. My careers adviser at school said that jobs would be hard to find, but I didn't realise just how hard until I was about

halfway through the course and I had to start thinking about jobs. I was in touch with past graduates who seemed to be either unemployed or doing completely unrelated work. I was keen on the idea of working in conservation, but I soon found out that I had chosen the most competitive area of all, and that most of the decisions in conservation are taken by managers, politicians and planners, rather than scientists.

My first job was with a science publishing firm, where I was really no more than a glorified secretary. I stuck that for about seven months, and then I was lucky enough to get a job with a pharmaceutical company as a lab assistant, which actually gave me useful experience. I spent a year there, meanwhile applying for every job I could find in the environmental field. I finally found this job, and I only got it because it is a very junior post that would normally be filled by a school leaver with four GCSEs. In a way I feel exploited because I'm being paid a pittance, much less than my qualifications deserve, but it seems the only way to do the work I want to do. I'm involved in research, and, while the work can be a bit routine at the moment, at least I have my foot in the door. Fortunately, I work with a good team of people who are giving me more responsibility than someone in this post would normally have, so for the first time since graduating I'm quite confident.

Paula is a scientific officer with a statutory conservation body, a job that she found soon after graduating three years ago.

I am the first to admit how lucky I am, and I could hardly believe it when I got this job because it was only the third that I had applied for, and it's exactly what I want. My post involves representing the organisation out in the field, which means a combination of public relations and politics. I travel around meeting private landowners, farmers, foresters, planners, and local government officials to talk about land management and to iron out any problems or conflicts of interest over our various protected areas. It can often be frustrating and bureaucratic, especially when you're dealing with public inquiries into threats to protected land, but, at the same time, it is very satisfying to know that you are putting conservation policy into practice. It is by no means a desk job, and I'm able to use my degree to good effect.

Chapter 9

Film-making, Photography and Writing

Introduction

Undoubtedly the most public and glamorous face of natural history (and, by extension, of conservation) is that of professional wildlife film-making. The success of TV series hosted by personalities like Sir David Attenborough and David Bellamy, the documentaries put out in BBC TV's 'The World About Us' slot and Anglia's 'Survival' slot, and the work of a generation of wildlife presenters have combined to give film-making an attraction that is, unfortunately, out of all proportion to the number of openings it offers.

Less well known, but also of considerable appeal, is the work of wildlife photographers and environmental writers. These are two career options that employ many conservationists and in which, with perseverance, those with the right abilities can make a full-time living.

Film-making

Britain has a long tradition of craftsmanship in wildlife film-making. A measure of the ability of many wildlife film-makers is that they make their work look so effortless and accessible that film-making seems easy. Nothing could be further from the truth.

Not only is the field competitive, but the work is demanding and arduous. The pleasure of working with film and of seeing a project through to completion is tempered by long hours of hard and sometimes tedious labour. Film-making is a career in which there are no easy options and no quick ways to the top.

That said, though, there are many people making wildlife films, and new film-makers will be needed in future. Jobs are available for those with very good qualifications.

Learning the Craft
Film-making involves both artistic and technical skills, and you should be sure that you possess these skills. The best way of getting started is to watch and absorb as many films as possible, noting the quality of the visual effects and how they were achieved - the editing, camera movements, lighting, sound effects, use of an on-screen or off-screen

narrator, and so on. Fortunately, wildlife films are common enough on television to make such a study possible.

At the same time, you should be experimenting with making films of your own. For this you will need either a good 9mm camera or a 16mm camera. Working with 16mm may be more expensive, but it brings you closer to the kind of situations and problems faced by professional film-makers, who work largely in that format. If possible, attend film-making classes and learn the theory from some of the many practical film-making guides that are available.

Once you understand the principles of film-making, you have the choice of either formal training at a college or film school (where you learn film-making as a craft and would be left to specialise in wildlife film-making in your own time) or a full-time job. Formal training is no guarantee of a job, but it does help because you can assess the job market from the inside.

Finding a Job

To find a job you will have to prove your ability, and few employers will consider you unless you have some of your own work to show. For that reason it is worth undertaking as many exercises and projects as you can, either alone or through your training centre. Keep filming and experimenting until you are sure that you have something worth showing. Be very critical of your work and be prepared to shoot a lot of wasted footage before you have a scene, a sequence or a complete exercise worth showing. Only a prodigy can come up with a winner first time around.

The job market is largely limited to television companies and independent film production companies. For television work the choice at the moment is BBC, ITV or Channel 4, and the normal point of entry is a post as a trainee in whatever field interests you. It could be editing, sound, lighting, camerawork, or working as a production assistant. Both BBC and ITV regularly recruit new trainees, but for every vacancy there are likely to be as many as 100 applicants. Those with proven interests and proven skills, but not necessarily experience, stand the best chance.

Once accepted by a television company it is a matter of working your way up through the normal internal promotion structure, proving your ability and expressing your interests. In most instances you should anticipate a long apprenticeship.

If you opt for work with a film production company, you have many more smaller organisations from which to choose. It may mean starting out in a menial or very junior post, and finding where the openings are likely to occur is a matter of keeping your ear to the ground. There are very few film production companies that specialise in wildlife film-making, but the field is changing all the time which means that opportunities vary.

Because the field is both changeable and competitive, it is difficult to generalise about careers in film-making. Although several thousand people are employed in film-making in the UK, few specialise in wildlife and these will take on other work as well. To succeed in film-making you should prove your abilities, be persistent and resilient, and enjoy a great deal of good luck.

Photography

Like film-making, photography demands both technical and artistic aptitudes, and although it is competitive it offers many more openings and outlets than film-making. Film-makers are restricted to working for television or film production companies, while photographers can sell their work to a host of magazines and journals, and to photo libraries, audo-visual companies, and galleries. It is also much easier and cheaper to set up with the right equipment. However, photography demands both ability and initiative.

Learning the Craft

Studying the work of other photographers, learning their techniques and carrying out your own experiments are essential. The basic tools are a good reflex camera (either 35mm or 2¼ square) and a range of lenses: at least a standard lens (50mm) and preferably a wide-angle lens (28mm), a medium telephoto (90-135mm) and a telephoto lens (200-600mm). As you become more specialised you will need specialist accessories such as remote controls, flash units, automatic winders, micro-focus lenses and extreme telephoto lenses.

You can teach yourself the basics of photography with advice from any of the many practical manuals and guides that exist. Otherwise, there are a number of part-time and full-time courses available at polytechnics, colleges of art and universities. All the courses will teach you the craft, but qualifications do not guarantee you employment.

Finding a Job

Photographers have two basic options: to work in either full-time or freelance employment. Full-time work is very difficult to find for the general photographer but even more so for someone wanting to specialise. A handful of journals employ wildlife photographers, but most buy photos in from freelances or photo libraries. A more realistic option is to work in a general capacity and pursue wildlife photography as a side-line or as just one aspect of the job.

Freelance work offers many more opportunities, but demands initiative, resilience and the ability to work alone. Most freelances sell their work through photo libraries or try to get commissioned work with a journal, a publisher, or an organisation that needs photographic material. It generally takes a great deal of time to become established, and for every photograph you sell you will have many rejected. You might lodge a large collection of photographs with a photo library and never make a sale, although you can guard against this by asking them which subjects are in most demand and where they have gaps that need filling.

It is difficult to make a living out of photography, particularly wildlife photography, but many manage to succeed, so the opportunities are there.

Writing

Writing is an artistic skill that has a longer and more finely developed heritage than either film-making or photography. To write successfully means you must have something to say and be able to express it in a succinct and effective manner. Conservation relies heavily on the printed word to convey the issues involved, and offers outlets for writers in journalism, information, education, press and public relations, and publicity.

Learning the Craft

Much can be learned from studying and imitating other writers. Writing well means being able to inform, entertain, educate, and even inspire readers, and demands not only an understanding of your topic but a wide general knowledge. To write well, you must have an interest in everything happening around you. Learning the skill means reading and writing copiously. For the environmental writer, it means understanding all the issues and knowing how to convey them to those who know about the subject and to those who do not.

An advantage is that the basic tools of the trade are cheap. Apart from paper and a word processor, many writers manage to exist with only a good dictionary, a thesaurus, and a copy of the *Writers' and Artists' Yearbook*.

Finding a Job

There are outlets for environmental writers in both the printed media (books, newspapers and journals) and the broadcast media (radio and television). Almost any organisation that wants to convey information will need to employ writers, either on a full-time or a freelance basis.

Full-time writers find a variety of work: writing for a periodical, running a press office, writing and publishing information material, putting together technical and practical manuals, or managing a press relations programme. Almost all the organisations mentioned in this book use writers in one capacity or another.

The freelance environmental field is already well subscribed, but there is always room for new writers. Making a living out of freelance work is not easy, especially for someone just starting out. Becoming established demands patience, resilience and application, and staying established demands a knowledge of the marketplace and the ability to offer a service. Most freelances derive their main income from regular commissioned work which comes from one or two main sources, and make up the balance from whatever else they can sell.

Case Studies

Sandy has spent the last three years working as a librarian in a photographic agency that specialises in wildlife subjects. It is less of a career for her than a regular job that allows her to pursue freelance wildlife photography in her own time. She has been taking photographs since she was five, encouraged by her father who owned his own photographic studio. She was regarded as unusual at school because there weren't many girls interested in photography as a hobby, let alone as a career. Her first job after leaving school was in her father's studio, after which she worked as a sales assistant in a camera shop, a job that didn't appeal to her.

> I had been trying to sell some of my work through various photo agencies, and made a couple of friends at the agency where I now work. They told me there was a vacancy for a librarian. I applied, and here I am. It's actually more fun than it sounds. I spend most of my time cataloguing photographs and sending selections out to clients, but I also work with wildlife photographers, going through their work and commissioning photographs. I get to talk to a lot of them about different techniques, and I try to get out every weekend and most evenings during the summer to take photos. I go for everything from general landscapes and habitats to plants, trees, flowers, mammals and birds. I have been experimenting recently with remote control flashlit photography of animals like badgers and pine martens, which has been an experience. I am gradually selling more and more of my work: to books, magazines, newspapers, and advertising and PR agencies. My greatest ambition is to have a book of my work published, but that's likely to be a few years off yet!

Chris is the assistant press officer for a national conservation charity. He began his working career after dropping out of art college and being offered a job as a copywriter with an advertising agency. It was a stop-gap job to give him time to think about a career. While he was copywriting he wrote to the charity for which he now works and offered to help them on a voluntary basis.

> I'd always been interested in their work and I just wanted to help somehow. They commissioned a few stories from me for their members' magazine, and when this job came up I applied and was lucky enough to get it. My copywriting experience helped a lot. I am enjoying the job enormously, especially as it gives me time to do a lot of freelance writing in the evenings and at weekends. I'm virtually running the press programme, writing press releases, features, leaflets, information packs, and the occasional audio-visual programme, as well as setting up press conferences and trying to get our activities covered in the press. My plan is to go freelance eventually, and live off writing and maybe a bit of photography. It's still too early, though, because you have to build up the contacts first. At the moment I'm concentrating on writing as much as I can and building up a portfolio.

Chapter 10

Working Overseas

Introduction

Because nature is not divided by national boundaries, there is a limit to how much individual nations acting alone can achieve in conservation. Birds migrate across the world, forests spread across many countries, rivers flow across continents, and oceans cover the planet. The creation of so many international conservation organisations over the past 30 years is some indication of how important international co-operation has become.

The need is particularly evident in the Third World, where governments face the greatest problems in balancing the conservation of their natural resources against the economic and social needs of their people. Most have tried to condense industrial revolutions that took hundreds of years in Europe into only a few decades, often with unforeseen and unfortunate side-effects.

Most Third World governments are now heavily in debt to the industrialised North for development aid in the form of capital, materials and education, and that aid has not always been appropriate to local needs. Dams have been built without the necessary research into river-flow characteristics; forests have been cleared to make way for agricultural projects unsuited to local soil and climatic conditions; improved medical care without parallel family planning has contributed to massive population growth; unequal land distribution has put too much pressure on agricultural land. The natural environment has suffered as a consequence, and the threat posed to tropical animal and plant species is just one of the negative results.

All this has meant that many of the most pressing environmental issues are to be found in the Third World, and temporary contract work or even permanent settlement abroad has many attractions for conservationists and environmental planners from the North. There are a number of opportunities available.

Working with a British Organisation

There are a number of British or British-based organisations that either study the problems of other countries or run active environmental and development aid projects abroad. Charities such as Oxfam, the World

Wide Fund for Nature (see Chapter 3) and the Fauna and Flora Preservation Society raise money for conservation projects abroad, and bodies such as the Overseas Development Administration, particularly the Natural Resources Institute (see Chapter 5) and the International Institute for Environment and Development concern themselves with Third World development issues. Many aid and natural resource management programmes are run through the Commonwealth and similar co-operative bodies.

Before approaching any of these bodies it is important to distinguish between those that offer openings within the United Kingdom only, and those that employ staff for overseas postings. Jobs that involve overseas travel are rare, very much in demand, and usually go only to candidates with a high level of relevant experience and qualifications.

Working with an International Organisation

There are a number of international organisations, based outside the UK, that conduct most of their business in English and frequently recruit people from the UK. These include United Nations agencies, such as the UN Environment Programme in Nairobi, the Food and Agriculture Organisation, multilateral development agencies such as the World Bank, and non-governmental organisations such as the International Union for Conservation of Nature and Natural Resources (IUCN) and the World Wide Fund for Nature in Switzerland. Other UN agencies of interest to environmentalists are listed in Chapter 14.

Vacancies in international organisations are not only highly sought-after, but are competed for by applicants from all over the world and the standards expected of them are generally high. You will need substantial relevant experience and qualifications, and it helps if you can speak another language (usually French or Spanish) and have lived or worked abroad before.

Working with a Voluntary Aid Agency

Taking part in voluntary aid programmes is an effective method of helping Third World communities learn to meet their economic and social needs, and therefore to manage and protect their environment. Britain currently sends about 800 volunteers overseas every year to some 50 countries. They are sent under the auspices of a variety of voluntary agencies: the four best known are the Catholic Institute for International Relations, Voluntary Service Overseas, Skillshare Africa (formerly International Voluntary Service) and the United Nations Association International Service.

Volunteers generally need to have useful skills and qualifications, mostly in agriculture, education, health services and crafts. Almost half the volunteers sent abroad are teachers. Skills needed by VSO in the field of natural resources are those of: agriculturalists, agronomists, farm managers, community agro/foresters, agricultural scientists, environmentalists, marine and freshwater fishery experts, horticulturalists and livestock specialists, as well as town planners and surveyors.

Applicants should be suitably qualified, aged over 21, in good health, and be willing to work for a minimum of two years at subsistence rates of pay or on a salary based on local rates. In the case of the Catholic Institute for International Relations, a UK allowance in addition to the overseas salary is also available, as well as free accommodation, flights, insurance, language training and a pre-departure grant. In general, only married couples with no dependent children are accepted, but VSO is now taking volunteers with dependants in certain skill shortfall areas. Details in *VSO and Dependants* (for VSO address, see p. 105). Recruitment is arranged nationally, and most of the agencies will supply applicants with information about current vacancies.

Many projects are aimed at increasing food production, improving community health, applying family planning, and helping rural communities to become self-sufficient. This kind of work provides anyone interested in conservation with useful experience and a perspective on problems faced by the Third World.

Undertaking Research Projects

A number of government and voluntary bodies run research programmes overseas, generally in a branch of life science or on some aspect of development aid. Most postings go to graduates in a related field who are already employed with the sponsoring organisation. The postings vary in their nature and duration; a project may last only a few weeks or, in the case of some British Antarctic Survey postings, can last three years, and demand the resilience to cope with living in close proximity to a small group of researchers for considerable periods in isolated and physically demanding conditions.

Alternatively, if you are lucky and have the right skills and qualifications, you could be invited to join a one-off conservation project or research expedition.

Emigrating or Settling Abroad

If you plan to travel or settle abroad for any length of time, the nature and scope of the options available to you change. Young people without particular skills, but with initiative, have been known to travel abroad and find work as rangers or guides in national parks, as members of local conservation groups, or as short-contract workers.

Planners and scientists with professional qualifications may find it relatively easy to be accepted as immigrants by countries such as Australia, Canada and New Zealand, where there are many openings in the environmental field, notably in national park and reserve management. Similarly, Third World countries often take on resource planners and managers for consultancy or contract work.

Perhaps the greatest number of career and further training opportunities are to be found in the United States. Resource management, particularly where it applies to forestry, soil, watershed, wildlife and range management, has a constant need for trained personnel, although the field is highly competitive.

Chapter 11

Finding and Applying for Jobs

Introduction

Environmental conservation has become such a popular career choice that there are not enough jobs to go around, and the competition for vacancies is stiff. Anyone who has tried writing to one of the many voluntary bodies, and has received a reply, will be only too familiar with such warnings.

On the other hand, it must be said that there *are* vacancies, that *someone* has to fill them, and that the well-prepared candidate is more likely to succeed than any other. One of the biggest problems that newcomers have had to face until now is the lack of accurate and informed career guidance. Conservationists themselves are often unaware of the range of careers the profession offers, and generally find it hard to offer any advice.

Looking for a job in conservation demands, above all, initiative. Remember that you are entering a profession where precedents are still being set, which can make it difficult to learn much from the examples of others who have gone before. It is still at the stage where the newcomer often has to make his or her own opportunities.

You will also need persistence, determination, and luck. Luck you cannot anticipate, but a few fundamental precautions will help you to find the job you want.

Know the Field

Many opportunities are missed because people do not fully understand what conservation involves and do not know what kind of people conservationists are. Newcomers tend to head instinctively for the wildlife organisations, because they are the best known and attract the most publicity. It is often a good idea to cast your net much wider and to look at jobs that involve other kinds of resource management and conservation. They all link up with one another in the end.

Know Your Interests

Once you have learned more about conservation you will be in a much better position to know which aspects interest you. Try not to specialise too early. Be prepared to consider any offers that come your way, because even the dullest post can teach you more about the job and can lead to better things.

Make Yourself Valuable

In our competitive world, specialist knowledge counts for a great deal, and even the most humble qualification can tip the scales in your favour if it makes you better than your competitors. You might know how to use a chainsaw or how to programme a computer. You might have a GCSE in zoology, a certificate earned from taking evening classes at a local college, or a university degree. It all helps.

Above all, though, you need experience, and conservation has the advantage over many other popular careers of offering unlimited opportunities for picking up voluntary unpaid experience. For just a few hours of your time you could learn how to manage a nature reserve, carry out a bird or mammal survey, run a publicity campaign, raise money, and more. Such experience will make you more familiar with conservation and more competitive when it comes to applying for a full-time job.

Know Where to Find the Jobs

It does no harm to send a letter to a conservation organisation asking about possible vacancies and enclosing your cv (and an sae), but most organisations receive many such letters. They rarely pay off, and many go unanswered altogether.

It makes much more sense to join some of the organisations that interest you and become actively involved, to subscribe to selected magazines and periodicals that are not available in your local library, and to keep an eye on all the newspapers and journals that carry job advertisements. The list of journals in Chapter 13 gives a general guide to sources of information on different careers and related vacancies.

Unfortunately, not all vacancies are advertised publicly, and some appointments are made internally. Joining conservation groups and meeting conservationists is the best way of keeping your ear to the ground.

Be Prepared and Persistent

You may land the ideal job on your first try, or you may go through endless applications without success, but with preparation and persistence the job you want must sooner or later come your way. Work carefully on your cv, putting in everything you think is relevant without being trivial, and presenting your case thoroughly, logically and neatly. Accept that you will have rejections, but turn each one to your advantage by learning from it and going into each successive application better prepared.

If you approach the job market realistically, stay aware of the competition, and try to strike the right note, you are bound to succeed eventually.

Future Prospects

New conservation bodies are being set up so frequently that directories of environmental groups are out of date almost before they are published. Governments are setting up new departments and research units to manage natural resources and monitor environmental laws. Training in conservation is now more widely available, and research and discussion are teaching us more about the natural world and the interdependence of life on earth.

The demand for jobs may be outstripping the opportunities at the moment but, as environmental management becomes more widely applied, so the openings will grow. The overall forecast is for growth in the scope and application of environmental conservation, greater professionalism in approaching the issues, and a corresponding growth in the number of career opportunities.

Part 2

Chapter 12

University and College Courses and Qualifications

Choosing a university or college course that prepares you for a career in environmental conservation is not straightforward. There are few courses in conservation or environmental management as such, and those that are available may not actually be the best for your purpose. There are no hard and fast rules, and it can be difficult to anticipate the needs of potential employers. Scientists and professional planners excepted, people working in conservation today come from a variety of backgrounds. In many cases they move into conservation through other jobs; in some cases, their specialist skills (eg languages, writing ability, computer skills) can be more important than their paper qualifications.

The most basic choice you need to make (assuming, that is, that you even want to take a college or university course) is whether you want to work in scientific or non-scientific conservation. When choosing a course, it helps if you know what you want to do with it eventually, how useful it will be in helping you to find a job, and how adaptable it will be (ie a specialist degree *may* limit your choice). On the whole, being a graduate is useful, but not always essential.

This chapter suggests a few course and subject ideas - some specialised, some more general. It doesn't list courses in journalism, law, geography or development studies, but these - and others - may often be just as useful. Before deciding which course suits you best, it is advisable to find out more about what each entails from the university or college concerned. Further details of courses are given in the *UCAS Handbook*, and *Directory of Courses in Land Based Industries*, £9.95 (inc postage), from the Association of Colleges in the Eastern Region, Merlin Place, Milton Road, Cambridge CB4 4DP.

The courses listed here do not include the many part-time and evening courses offered by colleges of further education and technical colleges, nor do they include vocational sandwich and part-time courses available to people already employed in conservation. Details of these are available from the various government, statutory, and professional bodies listed in Chapter 14.

Countryside Conservation and Management

Anglia Polytechnic University, Writtle College, Chelmsford, Essex CM1 3RR
3-year BSc(Hons) Rural Resource Development with option in wildlife and conservation
HND in Landscape and Amenity Management with option in Conservation in the Landscape
HND in Rural Resource Management with option in Habitat Conservation

Askham Bryan College, Askham Bryan, York YO2 3PR
BSc Land Management and Technology
BSc Hons Land Resources Management

Cheltenham and Gloucester College of Higher Education, The Park, Cheltenham, Gloucestershire GL50 2QF
BA/BA Hons modular degree scheme Countryside Planning with Environmental Policy

De Montfort University, The Gateway, Leicester LE1 9BH
BSc/BSc Hons Land Management

Edge Hill College of Higher Education, Ormskirk, Lancs L39 4QP
3-year BSc Single Hons Field Biology and Habitat Management

Harper Adams Agricultural College, Newport, Shropshire TF10 8NB
3-year BSc/BSc(Hons) Rural Environmental Protection

Liverpool John Moores University, Great Orford Street, Liverpool L3 5YD
3-year BSc/BSc Hons Countryside Management

North Riding College, Filey Road, Scarborough, North Yorkshire YO11 3AZ
3-year BSc Environmental Science and Conservation

Royal Agricultural College, Cirencester, Glos GL7 6JS
3-year BSc(Hons) Agriculture and Land Management, gives exemption from written exams of RICS for rural practice division

Silsoe College, Cranfield Institute of Technology, Silsoe, Bedford MK45 4DT
3-year BSc(Hons) Rural Environment Management
1-year MSc Land Resource Management
MSc Range Management
1-year MSc Soil Conservation
PGD Land Resource Planning
MSc Environmental Water Management

South Bank University, Borough Road, London SE1 0AA
3-year BSc/BSc Hons Estate Management

University College of North Wales, Bangor, Gwynedd LL57 2UW
3-year BSc Rural Resource Management
1-year MSc Rural Resource Management

University of Central England in Birmingham, Parry Barr, Birmingham B42 2SU
3-year BSc/BSc Hons Environmental Planning with Natural Resource Management
Estate Management

University of Central Lancashire, Newton Rigg College (formerly Cumbria College of Agriculture and Forestry), Penrith
HND Environmental Land Management

University of East London, Barking Campus, Longbridge Road, Dagenham, Essex RM8 2AS
BSc/BSc Hons Land Management

University of Humberside; course available only at Bishop Burton College of Agriculture, Beverley
BSc (Hons) Countryside Management
HND Countryside Management

University of Plymouth, Seale-Hayne Campus, Newton Abbot, Devon TQ12 6NQ
2-year HND Rural Resource Management
3-year full-time BSc(Hons) Agriculture and Countryside Management
3-year BSc(Hons) Rural Resource Management

Faculty of Urban and Regional Studies, University of Reading, Whiteknights, Reading RG6 2AH
3-year BSc Rural Land Management (specialisation in Rural Studies)
3-year BSc(Hons) Rural Land Management, taught at the Royal Agricultural College, Circencester, gives exemption from written exams of RICS for Rural Practice Division
3-year BSc(Hons) Rural Resource Management
3-year MPhil/AD Land Management

University of Sussex, Sussex House, Falmer, Brighton BN1 9RH
3-year BSc Hons Ecology and Conservation

University of London, Wye, Ashford, Kent TN25 5AH
3-year BSc/BSc(Hons) Countryside Management
1-year MSc Conservation of Soil Fertility
1-year MSc Landscape Ecology, Design and Management
1-year MSc Rural Resources and Environmental Policy

University of Wales, Aberystwyth, Dyfed, DY23 2AX
3-year BA Environmental Planning and Management
3-year BSc(Hons) Rural Resource Management

University of Newcastle upon Tyne, Newcastle upon Tyne, NE1 7RU
3-year BSc(Hons) Countryside Management
3-year BSc(Hons) Rural Resource Management
3-year BSc(Hons) Natural Resources
3-year BSc(Hons) in Terrestrial Ecology

The University of York, Heslington, York YO1 5DD
3-year BSc Hons Ecology, Conservation and Environment
3-year BSc Hons Environmental Economics and Environmental Management

Welsh Agricultural College, Llanbadarn Fawr, Aberystwyth, Dyfed SY23 3AL
3-year BSc/HND Countryside Management

Napier University, 219 Colinton Road, Edinburgh EH14 1DJ
3-year BSc/BSc Hons Rural Resources with transfer possible to HND programme
HND Rural Resource Management

The Scottish Agricultural College (Edinburgh, Aberdeen, Ayr), Academic Registry, Freepost, Ayr KA6 5HW
3/4-year BSc/BSc(Hons) in Rural Resources

University of Aberdeen, Department of Agriculture, 581 King Street, Aberdeen AB9 1UD
4-year BSc in Countryside and Environmental Management

The University of Stirling, Stirling FK9 4LA
3-year BSc Conservation Management

Other Environmental and Management Courses

Bedford College of Higher Education, Cauldwell Street, Bedford MK40 2BZ
3-year BA(Hons) Environmental Studies

Cheltenham and Gloucester College of Higher Education, Department of Countryside and Landscape, Faculty of Environment and Leisure, Francis Close Hall, Swindon Road, Cheltenham, Glos GL50 4AZ
3-year BA(Hons) Countryside Planning

Gwent College of Higher Education, Alltyn Avenue, Newport, Gwent NP9 5XA
3-year BA (University of Wales) in Combined Studies with option in Environmental Studies

Kingston University, Penryhn, Kingston upon Thames KT1 2EE
3-year Science Modular Degree Scheme, Resources and the Environment

Liverpool Institute of Higher Education, St Katherine's College, Stand Park Road, Liverpool L16 8ND
3-year BA(Hons) or BSc(Hons) Combined Studies with option in Environmental Studies

Liverpool John Moores University, Rodney House, 70 Mount Pleasant, Liverpool L3 5UX
3-year BSc/BSc(Hons) Integrated Credit Scheme – named routes include countryside management, earth science
3-year BA/BA(Hons) Combined Studies Integrated Credit Scheme; named routes include Urban Planning

Manchester Metropolitan University, All Saints, Manchester M15 6BH
3-year BSc/BSc(Hons) Combined Studies, with option in Environmental Studies
3-year BSc/BSc(Hons) Environmental Management

Manchester Metropolitan University, Crewe and Alsager College Faculty, Crewe Road, Crewe, Cheshire CW1 1DU
3-year BSc Combined Studies (Environmental Studies)

Otley College of Agriculture and Horticulture, Ipswich, Suffolk IP6 9EY
1-year postgraduate certificate in Environmental Interpretation
1-year postgraduate certificate in Habitat Management
1-year postgraduate certificate in Woodland Management
1-year postgraduate certificate in Conservation Management

University College of North Wales, Bangor, Gwynedd LL57 2UW
1-year MSc in Environmental Forestry

University of Central Lancashire, Preston, Lancashire PR1 2TQ
3-year BSc/BSc(Hons) Combined Honours with option in Environmental Management

University of Derby, Kedleston Road, Derby DE22 1GB

3-year BSc(Hons) Environmental Monitoring
3-year BA(Hons) Modular Scheme with option in Environmental Studies
3-year BSc(Hons) Environmental Studies

University of East London, Longbridge Road, Dagenham, Essex RM8 2AS
3-year BA/BA(Hons) in Combined Studies with option in Environmental Studies

University of Hertfordshire, College Lane, Hatfield, Herts AL10 9AB
3-year BSc(Hons) Environmental Studies

University of Hull, Hull HU6 7RX
3-year BSc(Hons) Environmental and Resource Management

University of London, Wye College, Ashford, Kent TN25 5AH
3-year BSc/BSc(Hons) Agriculture and the Environment
3-year BSc/BSc(Hons) in Rural Environment Studies
1-year MSC in Rural Resources and Environmental Policy

University of Northumbria at Newcastle, Ellison Building, Ellison Place, Newcastle upon Tyne NE1 8ST
3-year BSc(Hons) Environmental Studies

University of Nottingham, University Park, Nottingham NG7 2RD
3-year BSc Environmental Science in Agriculture

University of Reading, Faculty of Urban and Regional Studies, Whiteknights, Reading RG6 2BU
2-year MPhil/AD in Environmental Planning

University of Sunderland, Langham Tower, Ryhope Road, Sunderland SR2 7EE
3-year BSc/BSc(Hons) Environmental Studies

West London Institute of Higher Education, Gordon House, 300 St Margaret's Road, Twickenham TW1 1PT
3-year BSc/BSc(Hons) Modular Degree Scheme with option in Geography and Environmental Issues

Worcester College of Higher Education, Henwick Grove, Worcester WR2 6AJ
BSc(Hons) Environmental Management

Science and Applied Science

Bath College of Higher Education, Newton Park, Newton St Loe, Bath BA2 9BN
3-year BA(Hons)/BSc(Hons) Combined Studies with option in Environmental Biology

Coventry University, Priory Street, Coventry CV1 5FB
3-year BSc(Hons) Environmental Science

De Montfort University, The Gateway, Leicester LE1 9BH
3-year BSc/BSc(Hons) Science and the Environment

Imperial College of Science, Technology and Medicine (University of London), South Kensington, London SW7 2AZ
BSc in Ecology or Plant Science, with common first year or part year, with Associateship of the Royal College of Science

Lancaster University, Lancaster LA1 4YW
BSc(Hons) Ecology
BSc(Hons) Environmental Science

Manchester Metropolitan University, All Saints, Manchester M15 6BH
3/4-year BSc/BSc(Hons) Environmental Science

Middlesex University, Trent Park, Cockfosters Road, Barnet, Herts EN4 0PT
3-year BSc(Hons) Applied Environmental Science

Nene College, Moulton Park, Northampton NN2 7AL
3-year BA(Hons)BSc(Hons) in Combined Studies with option in Environmental Biology

Otley College of Agriculture and Horticulture, Ipswich, Suffolk IP6 9EY
1-year postgraduate certificate in Biological Surveying
1-year postgraduate certificate in Environmental Interpretation
1-year course (no qualification) in Environmental Science

Oxford Brookes University, Headington, Oxford OX3 0BP
3-year BSc/BSc(Hons) Environmental Biology

Roehampton Institute of Higher Education, Roehampton Lane, London SW15 5PU
3-year BA(Hons)/BSc(Hons) in Combined Studies with option in Environmental Studies

Sheffield Hallam University, Pond Street, Sheffield S1 1WB
3-year BA/BA(Hons) in Combined Studies with option in Environmental Studies

South Bank University, Borough Road, London SE1 0AA
BSc/BSc Hons Environmental Biology

Staffordshire University, College Road, Stoke-on-Trent, Staffordshire ST4 2DE
3-year BSc/BSc(Hons) Environmental Studies
3-year BSc/BSc(Hons) Applied Science Programme with option in Environmental Science

University College of North Wales, Bangor, Gwynedd LL57 2UW
3-year BSc in Crop and Soil Science
3-year BSc in Soil and Forest Science
3-year BSc Water Resources
3-year BSc in Wood Science
3-year BSc(Hons) in Environmental Science

University of Bath, School of Biological Sciences, Claverton Down, Bath BA2 7AY
1-year MSc in Environmental Science, Policy and Planning

University of Brighton, Brighton, Sussex BN2 4AT
3-year BSc(Hons) Environmental Science

University of Central Lancashire, Preston, Lancashire PR1 2TQ
3-year BSc/BSc(Hons) Combined Honours with options in biochemistry and environmental management

University of Greenwich, Wellington Street, Woolwich, London SE18 6PF
3-year BSc/BSc(Hons) Applied Sciences with option in Earth Sciences and Environmental Science
3-year BSc(Hons) Environmental Earth Sciences

3-year BSc/BSc(Hons) Environmental Biology
3-year BSc/BSc(Hons) Environmental Control

University of Glamorgan Prifysgol Morgannwg, Treforest, Pontypridd, Mid-Glamorgan
3-year BSc/BSc(Hons) option in Environmental Pollution Science

University of London, Wye College, Ashford, Kent TN25 5AH
3-year BSc/BSc(Hons) in Environmental Science
3-year BSc/BSc(Hons) in Plant Sciences
1-year MSc in Plant Biotechnology
1-year MSc in Tropical and Subtropical Horticulture and Crop Science
1-year MSc in Applied Plant Sciences
1-year MSc in Conservation of Soil Fertility

University of Newcastle upon Tyne, Newcastle upon Tyne NE1 7RU
3-year BSc(Hons) Agricultural and Environmental Science
3-year BSc(Hons) in Environmental Biology
3-year BSc(Hons) in Soil Science
1 or 2-year MSc or Diploma in Soil Science
1 or 2-year MSc or Diploma in Tropical Agricultural and Environmental Science

University of North London, Holloway Road, London N7 8DB
3-year BSc/BSc(Hons) Environmental and Ecological Chemistry
3-year BSc/BSc(Hons) Environmental Science
3-year BSc/BSc(Hons) Ecological Science

University of Nottingham School of Agriculture, Sutton Bonington, Nr Loughborough, Leicestershire LE12 5RD
3-year BSc in Agricultural Biochemistry

University of Portsmouth, University House, Winston Churchill Avenue, Portsmouth PO1 2UP
BSc/BSc Hons Environmental Science

University of Reading, Department of Agriculture, Earley Gate, PO Box 236, Reading RG6 2AT
3-year BSc(Hons) in Soils and the Environment
1-year postgraduate diploma in Tropical Agricultural Development
2-year MAgrSc in Tropical Agricultural Development
2-year MPhil in Agricultural Botany
1-year MSc in Soil Science
1-year MSc in Tropical Agricultural Development

University of Sunderland, Langham Tower, Ryhope Road, Sunderland SR2 7EE
3-year BSc(Hons) in Environmental Biology

University of Wolverhampton, Wulfruna Street, Wolverhampton WV1 1SB
3-year BSc/BSc(Hons) Applied Sciences with option in Environmental Science

University of Surrey, Guildford, Surrey GU2 5XH
3/4-year BSc(Hons) Environmental Microbiology

Worcester College of Higher Education, Henwick Grove, Worcester WR2 6AJ
3-year BSc(Hons) Environmental Science

University of Aberdeen, Department of Agriculture, 581 King Street, Aberdeen AB9 1UD
4-year BSc in Crop and Soil Sciences

University of Edinburgh, Edinburgh EH8 9YL
4-year BSc(Hons) in Agricultural Science (Crop and Soil Science)
4-year BSc(Hons) in Ecological Sciences

University of Glasgow, Glasgow G12 8QQ
4-year BSc(Hons) in Aquatic Bioscience

The Queen's University of Belfast, Newforge Lane, Belfast BT7 1NN
3-year BSc in Applied Plant Science
BSc/BAgr in Agricultural Science
3/4-year BSc(Hons) in Environmental Biology

Forestry

University College of North Wales, Bangor, Gwynedd LL57 2DG
3/4-year BSc(Hons) in Agroforestry
3/4-year BSc(Hons) in Forestry
3-year BSc(Hons) in Forestry and Forestry Products
3-year BSc in Soil and Forest Science
3-year BSc in Wood Science
1-year MSc in Environmental Forestry
1-year MSc in Forest Industries Technology

University of Central Lancashire, Preston PR1 2HE at Newton Rigg College, Cumbria, and Myerscough College
BSc Forestry

University of Oxford, Dept of Plant Sciences, South Parks Road, Oxford OX1 3RB
1-year MSc Forestry and its relation to Land Use

University of Edinburgh, Division of Biological Sciences, Institute of Ecology and Resource Management, West Mains Road, Edinburgh EH9 3JG
4-year BSc(Hons) Agriculture Forestry and Rural Economy
4-year BSc(Hons) Forestry

Landscape Architecture

Anglia Polytechnic University, Writtle College, Chelmsford, Essex CM1 3RR
BSc/BSc Hons Landscape and Garden Design

University of Central England in Birmingham, Perry Barr, Birmingham B42 2SU
BA/BA Hons Landscape Architecture

Cheltenham and Gloucester College of Higher Education, PO Box 220, The Park, Cheltenham, Glos GL50 4QF
4-year BA(Hons)/Dip in Landscape Architecture

University of Greenwich, Wellington Street, Woolwich, London SE18 6PF
BA/BA Hons Landscape Architecture

Leeds Metropolitan University, Landscape Architecture, School of the Environment, Brunswick Building, Leeds LS2 8BU
3-year BA(Hons)/Dip in Landscape Architecture

Manchester Metropolitan University, Manchester M15 6BH
3-year BA(Hons)/Dip Landscape Design

University of London, Wye College, Wye, Ashford, Kent TN25 5AH
MSc in Landscape Ecology, Design and Maintenance

University of Reading, PO Box 217, Reading, Berkshire RG6 2AH
BSc in Landscape Management

University of Sheffield, Department of Landscape Architecture, Sheffield S10 2TN
4-year BSc(Hons) including possible Diploma year
Landscape Design and Plant Science

Heriot-Watt University, Faculty of Environmental Studies, Lauriston Place, Edinburgh EH3 9DF
3-year BA(Hons) in Landscape Architecture

Town and Country Planning

University of Central England in Birmingham, Perry Barr, Birmingham B42 2SU
4-year BSc(Hons) and Diploma in Environmental Planning Studies

Bristol University of the West of England, Frenchay Campus, Coldharbour Lane, Bristol BS16 1QY
4-year BA(Hons) in Town and Country Planning

Oxford Brookes University, School of Planning, Headington, Oxford OX3 0BP
4-year BA(Hons) with Diploma in Planning Studies gives exemption from RTPI professional examinations

Sheffield Hallam University, Pond Street, Sheffield S1 1WB
3-year BA/BA(Hons) in combined studies with option in Planning Studies/ Town Planning and Urban Studies

South Bank University, Department of Planning, Housing and Development, Wandsworth Road, London SW8 2JZ
BA(Hons) in Town Planning

University of Manchester, Department of Planning and Landscape, Manchester M13 9PL
4-year BA(Hons) in Town and Country Planning

University of Newcastle upon Tyne, Department of Town and Country Planning, Claremont Tower, Claremont Road, Newcastle upon Tyne NE1 7RU
5-year BA(Hons) in Town Planning

The Queen's University of Belfast, School of Architecture and Planning, 2 Lennoxvale, Belfast BT9 5BY
4-year BSc in Environmental Planning

University of Sheffield, Department of Town and Regional Planning, Sheffield S10 2TN
4-year BA in Urban Studies

University of Wales, College of Cardiff, Aberconway Building, Colum Drive, Cardiff CF1 3YN
5-year BSc and Diploma in City and Regional Planning

University of Westminster, School of Urban Development and Planning, 35 Marylebone Road, London NW1 5LS
4-year BA(Hons) in Urban Studies

Heriot-Watt University, Department of Planning and Housing, Lauriston Place, Edinburgh EH3 9DF
5-year BSc(Hons) in Town Planning

University of Dundee, Department of Town and Regional Planning, Perth Road, Dundee DD1 4HT
4-year BSc(Hons) in Town and Regional Planning

University of Strathclyde, Centre for Planning, 50 Richmond Street, Glasgow G1 1XN
4-year BA(Hons) in Planning

Chapter 13

Useful Journals

There are numerous journals that deal with conservation and the natural environment. The most important are listed in this chapter. Some journals carry job advertisements, but they are included here principally because they give the best coverage of their topics and are useful sources of news and information.

Journals

Conservation and Natural History
BBC Wildlife Magazine
BBC Publications and Wildlife Publications, Broadcasting House, Whiteladies Road, Bristol BS8 2LR; 0272 732211. Monthly.

Birds
Royal Society for the Protection of Birds, The Lodge, Sandy, Bedfordshire SG12 2DL; 0767 680551. Quarterly.

The Conserver
British Trust for Conservation Volunteers, 36 St Mary's Street, Wallingford, Oxfordshire OX10 0EU; 0491 39766. Quarterly.

Country-Side
British Naturalists Association, 48 Russell Way, Higham Ferrers, Northampton; 0933 314672. Four issues per year.

Green Drum
18 Colton Lake Road, Birmingham B45 8PL; 021-445 2576. Quarterly.

Green Magazine
The Northern and Shell Building, PO Box 381 Millharbour, London E14 9TW; 071-987 5090.

The Living Countryside
Eaglemoss Publications, Rose Court, Mill Lane, Crondall, Farnham, Surrey GU10 5RR; 0252 850000. Weekly.

The National Trust
National Trust, 36 Queen Anne's Gate, London SW1H 0AS; 071-222 9251. Three issues per year.

Natural World
The Illustrated London News, Sea Containers House, 20 Upper Ground, London SE1 9PF; 071-928 2111. Three issues per year.

Oryx
Blackwell Scientific Publications, Osney Mead, Oxford OX2 0EL;
0865 240201. Quarterly.

Trends in Ecology and Evolution
Elsevier Trends Journals, 68 Hills Road, Cambridge CB2 1LA;
0223 315961. Monthly.

Wildfowl & Wetlands
The Wildfowl and Wetlands Trust, The New Grounds, Slimbridge,
Gloucestershire GL2 7BT; 0453 890333. Two issues per year.

WWF News
World Wide Fund for Nature, Panda House, Weyside Park, Godalming, Surrey
GU7 1XR; 048342 6444. Quarterly, newspaper format.

Environment

Countryside Campaigner
Council for the Protection of Rural England, Greenlines Publications Ltd,
164 Barkby Road, Leicester LE4 7LE; 0533 460722. Three issues per year.

The Ecologist
Agriculture House, Bath Road, Sturminster Newton, Dorset
OT10 1OU; 0258 73476. Bi-monthly.

Econews
Green Party, 10 Station Parade, Balham High Road, London SW12 9AZ;
081-673 0045. Six issues per year.

Journal of Ecology
Blackwell Scientific Publications Ltd, Osney Mead, Oxford OX2 0EL;
0865 240201. Quarterly.

Resurgence
Resurgence Trust, Ford House, Hartland, Bideford, Devon EX39 6EE;
0237 441293. Bi-monthly.

Resource Management

Commonwealth Forestry Review
Commonwealth Forestry Association, South Parks Road, Oxford OX1 3RB; 0865
275072. Quarterly.

Forestry
Oxford University Press, Journals Department, Walton Street, Oxford OX2 6DP;
0865 56767. Four issues per year.

Landscape Design
13a West Street, Reigate, Surrey RH2 9BL; 0737 225374.

The Planner
179 Kings Cross Road, London WC1X 9BZ; 071-833 9111. Fortnightly.

Quarterly Journal of Forestry
Royal Forestry Society of England, Wales and Northern Ireland, 102 High Street,
Tring, Hertfordshire HP23 4AH; 044282 2028. Quarterly.

Resources Policy
Butterworth-Heinemann Companies, Linacre House, Jordan Hill, Oxford OX2
8DP; 0865 310366.

Scottish Forestry
Royal Scottish Forestry Society, 11 Atholl Crescent, Edinburgh EH9 8HE; 031-229 8180. Quarterly.

Town & Country Planning
Town & Country Planning Association, 17 Carlton House Terrace, London SW1Y 5AS; 071-930 8903. Monthly.

World Water
Thomas Telford Ltd, Thomas Telford House, 1 Heron Quay, London E14 9XF; 071-987 6999. Monthly.

Science

The Biochemical Journal
Portland Press, 59 Portland Place, London W1N 3AJ; 071-580 5530. Bi-monthly.

Biological Conservation
Elsevier Applied Science Publishers, Crown House, Linton Road, Barking, Essex IG11 8JU. 081-594 7272. Monthly.

Biologist
Institute of Biology, 20 Queensberry Place, London SW7 2DZ; 071-581 8333. Five issues per year.

Journal of Animal Ecology
Blackwell Scientific Publications Ltd, Osney Mead, Oxford OX2 0EL; 0865 240201. Three issues per year.

Journal of Applied Ecology
Blackwell Scientific Publications Ltd, Osney Mead, Oxford OX2 0EL; 0865 240201. 3 issues per year.

Journal of Biological Education
Institute of Biology, 20 Queensberry Place, London SW7 2DZ; 071-581 8333. Quarterly.

Journal of Ecology
Blackwell Scientific Publications Ltd, Osney Mead, Oxford OX2 0EL; 0865 240201. Quarterly.

Journal of Natural History
Taylor & Francis Ltd, 4 John Street, London WC1N 2ET; 071-405 2237. Bi-monthly.

Journal of the Marine Biological Association
Cambridge University Press, The Edinburgh Building, Shaftesbury Road, Cambridge CB2 2RU; 0223 312393. Quarterly.

Journal of Zoology
Oxford Journals, Pinkhill House, Southfield Road, Eynsham, Oxford OX8 1JJ; 0865 882283. Monthly.

Mammal Review
Blackwell Scientific Publications Ltd, Osney Mead, Oxford OX2 0EL; 0865 240201. Quarterly.

Marine Environmental Research
Elsevier Applied Science Publishers, Crown House, Linton Road, Barking, Essex IG11 8JU; 081-594 7272. Eight issues per year.

Marine Pollution Bulletin
Pergamon Journals Ltd, Headington Hill Hall, Oxford OX3 0BW; 0865 794141. 24 issues per year.

Nature
Macmillan Magazines, 4 Little Essex Street, London WC2R 3LF; 071-836 6633. Weekly.

New Scientist
IPC Holborn Publishing Group, King's Reach Tower, Stamford Street, London SE1 9LS; 071-261 5000. Weekly.

Global Issues

New Internationalist
New Internationalist Publications Ltd, 55 Rectory Road, Oxford OX4 1BW; 0865 728181. Monthly.

Third World Planning Review
Liverpool University Press, PO Box 147, Liverpool L69 3BX; 051-794 2237. Quarterly.

Third World Quarterly
Carfax Publishing Co, PO Box 25, Abingdon, Oxon OX14 3UE; 0235 555335. Quarterly.

Urban Focus
Civic Trust, 17 Carlton House Terrace, London SW1Y 5AW; 071-930 0914. Quarterly.

World Development
Pergamon Press Ltd, Headington Hill Hall, Oxford OX3 0BW; 0865 794141. Monthly.

Foreign Journals

Environmental Management
Springer-Verlag New York Inc, 175 Fifth Avenue, New York, NY 10010, USA. Bi-monthly.

Sierra
Sierra Club, 730 Polk Street, San Francisco, California 94109, USA.

Smithsonian
Arts and Industries Building, 900 Jefferson Drive, Washington DC 20560, USA.

Chapter 14

Useful Addresses

Listed in this chapter are the addresses of many organisations referred to in Part 1, together with those of other relevant and related bodies. Some are potential employers, some accept members and voluntary assistance, some are professional institutes; all are useful sources of further information on different aspects of conservation. When writing to the voluntary bodies, it helps to enclose a stamped addressed envelope.

Voluntary Bodies

British Association of Landscape Industries
9 Henry Street, Keighley, West Yorkshire BD21 3DR; 0535 606139

British Association of Nature Conservationists
PO Box 14, Neston, South Wirral, Merseyside L94 7UP

British Trust for Conservation Volunteers
36 St Mary's Street, Wallingford, Oxfordshire OX10 0EU; 0491 39766

British Trust for Ornithology
The Nunnery, Nunnery Place, Thetford, Norfolk IP24 2PU; 0842 750050

Centre for Alternative Technology
Machynlleth, Powys SY20 9AZ; 0654 702400

Civic Trust
17 Carlton House Terrace, London SW1Y 5AW; 071-930 0914

Conservation Trust
National Environment Education Centre, George Palmer Site, Northumberland Avenue, Reading RG2 7PW; 0734 868442

Council for National Parks
246 Lavender Hill, London SW11 1LJ; 071-924 4044

Council for the Protection of Rural England
Warwick House, 25 Buckingham Palace Road, London SW1W 0PP; 071-976 6433

English Heritage
23 Savile Row, London W1X 2HE; 071-973 3000

The Environment Council
80 York Way, London N1 9AG; 071-278 4736

Environmental Investigation Agency
2 Pear Tree Court, London EC1R 0DS; 071-490 7040

Friends of the Earth
26-28 Underwood Street, London N1 7JQ; 071-490 1555

Greenpeace Environmental Trust
Canonbury Villas, London N1 2PN; 071-354 5100

Henry Doubleday Research Association
Ryton Gardens, Ryton-on-Dunsmore, Coventry CB8 3LG; 0203 303517

Marine Conservation Society
9 Gloucester Road, Ross-on-Wye, Herefordshire HR9 5BU; 0989 66017

National Society for Clean Air
136 North Street, Brighton, Sussex BN1 1RG; 0273 26313

National Trust
36 Queen Anne's Gate, London SW1H 9AS; 071-222 9251

National Trust for Ireland
Tailor's Hall, Back Lane, Dublin 2, Republic of Ireland; 353 (1) 541786

National Trust for Scotland
5 Charlotte Square, Edinburgh EH2 4DU; 031-226 5922

Organic Growers Association
86 Colston Street, Bristol BS1 5BB; 0272 299800

Population Concern
231 Tottenham Court Road, London WC1P 9AE; 071-387 0455

Royal Society for the Protection of Birds
The Lodge, Sandy, Bedfordshire SG19 2DL; 0767 680551

RSNC The Wildlife Trusts Partnership
The Green, Wickham Park, Lincoln LN5 5RR; 0522 544400

Scottish Civic Trust
24 George Square, Glasgow G2 1EF; 041-221 1466

Scottish Wildlife Trust Ltd
Cramond House, Kirk Cramond, Cramond Glebe Road, Edinburgh EH4 6NS; 031-312 7765

Soil Association Ltd
86-88 Colston Street, Bristol BS1 5BB; 0272 290661

The Tidy Britain Group
The Pier, Wigan WN3 4EX; 0942 824620

Tree Council
35 Belgrave Square, London SW1X 8QN; 071-235 8854

Whale & Dolphin Conservation Society
19a James Street West, Bath, Avon BA1 2BT; 0225 334511

Wild Flower Society
68 Outwood Road, Loughborough, Leicestershire LE11 3LY; 0509 215598

Wildfowl and Wetlands Trust
The New Grounds, Slimbridge, Gloucestershire GL2 7BT; 0453 890333

Woodland Trust
Autumn Park, Dysart Road, Grantham, Lincolnshire NG31 6LL; 0476 74297

WWF UK (World Wide Fund for Nature)
Panda House, Weyside Park, Godalming, Surrey GU7 1BR; 048342 6444

Resource Management

British Wind Energy Association
4 Hamilton Place, London W1V 0BQ; 0753 882447

Institute of Chartered Foresters
7A Colme Street, Edinburgh EH3 6AA; 031-225 2705

Landscape Institute
6-7 Barnard Mews, London SW11 1QU; 071-738 9166

Network for Alternative Technology and Technology Assessment (NATTA)
c/o Energy and Environment Research Unit, Faculty of Technology, The Open University, Walton Hall, Milton Keynes MK7 6AA

Royal Forestry Society
102 High Street, Tring, Hertfordshire HP23 4AH; 0442 822028

Royal Institution of Chartered Surveyors
Rural Practice Division, 12 Great George Street
Parliament Square, London SW1P 3AD; 071-222 7000

Royal Scottish Forestry Society
11 Atholl Crescent, Edinburgh EH9 8HE; 031-229 8180

Royal Town Planning Institute
26 Portland Place, London W1N 4BE; 071-636 9107

Timber Growers United Kingdom Ltd
Agriculture House, Knightsbridge, London SW1X 7NJ; 071-235 2925

Water Authorities Association
1 Queen Anne's Gate, London SW1H 9BT; 071-222 8111

Government Bodies

Agricultural Development and Advisory Service
MAFF, Victory House, 30-34 Kingsway, London WC2B 6TU; 071-405 4310

Agricultural Scientific Services Station
East Craigs, Corstorphine, Edinburgh EH12 8NJ; 031-556 8400

British Antarctic Survey
High Cross, Madingley Road, Cambridge CB3 0ET; 0223 311354

British Geological Survey
London Information Desk
Geological Museum, Exhibition Road, London SW7; 071-589 4090

Department for Education
Sanctuary Buildings, Great Smith Street, London SW1P 3BT; 071-925 5000

Department of the Environment
2 Marsham Street, London SW1P 3EB; 071-276 3000

Energy Efficiency Office
1 Palace Street, London SW1E 5HE; 071-238 3000

102 Careers in Environmental Conservation

Farming and Wildlife Advisory Group
National Agricultural Centre, Stoneleigh, Kenilworth CV8 2RX; 0203 696699

Forestry Commission
231 Corstorphine Road, Edinburgh EH12 7AT; 031-334 0303

Forestry and Arboricultural Safety and Training Council
231 Corstorphine Road, Edinburgh EH12 7AT; 031-334 8083

Natural Environment Research Council
Polaris House, North StarAvenue, Swindon SW2 1EU; 0793 411500

Recruitment and Assessment Services, Civil Service
Alençon Link, Basingstoke, Hampshire RG21 1JB; 0256 29222

Statutory Bodies

Countryside Commission
John Dower House, Crescent Place, Cheltenham, Gloucestershire GL50 3RA; 0242 521381

Scottish Natural Heritage (Training)
Battleby, Redgorton, Perth PH1 3EW; 0738 27921

English Nature
Northminster House, Peterborough PE1 1UA; 0733 340345

Education and Research

Council for Environmental Education
University of Reading, London Road, Reading, Berkshire RG1 5AQ; 0734 756061

Countryside Council for Wales
Plas Penrhos, Ffordd Penrhos, Bangor, Gwynedd LL57 2LQ; 0248 370444

Field Studies Council
Preston Montford, Montford Bridge, Shrewsbury, Shropshire SY4 1HW; 0743 850674

National Rivers Authority
30-34 Albert Embankment, London SE1 4TL; 071-820 0101

Scottish Field Studies Association Ltd
Kindrogan Field Centre, Enochdhn, Blairgowrie, Perthshire PH10 7PG; 0250 881286

Scottish Natural Heritage (Recruitment)
12 Hope Terrace, Edinburgh EH9 2AS; 031-447 4784

UCAS (Universities & Colleges Admissions Service)
Fulton House, Jessop Avenue, Cheltenham, Gloucestershire GL50 3SH; 0242 222444

Science Bodies

British Ecological Society
Burlington House, Piccadilly, London W1V 0LQ; 071-434 2641

Institute of Biology
20 Queensberry Place, London SW7 2DZ; 071-581 8333

Institution of Environmental Sciences
14 Prince's Gate, London SW7 1PU; 071-766 6755

Royal Horticultural Society
Vincent Square, London SW1P 2PE; 071-834 4333. Hon Secretary: 0252 515511

Zoological Society of London
Zoological Gardens, Regent's Park, London NW1 4RY; 071-722 3333

International Interest

Catholic Institute for International Relations
Unit 3 Canonbury Yard, 190A New North Road, London N1 7BJ; 071-354 0883

Centre for World Development Education
1 Catton Street, London WC1R 4AB; 071-831 3844

Commonwealth Secretariat
Marlborough House, London SW1Y 5HX; 071-839 3411

Earthscan
120 Pentonville Road, London N1 9JN; 071-278 0433

International Farm Experience Programme
Young Farmers' Clubs Centre, National Agricultural Centre, Stoneleigh, Kenilworth CV8 2LG; 0203 696584

International Institute for Environment and Development
3 Endsleigh Street, London WC1H 0DD; 071-388 2177

International Planned Parenthood Federation
Regents College, Regent's Park, London NW1 4NS; 071-486 0741

National Council for Voluntary Organisations
Regents Wharf, All Saints Road, London N1 9RL; 071-713 6161

Overseas Development Administration
Esso House, Victoria Street, London SW1E 5JW; 071-917 7000

Overseas Development Natural Resources Institute
56 Grays Inn Road, London WC1X 8LT; 071-405 7943

Panos Institute
9 White Lion Street, London N1 9PD; 071-278 1111

Population Concern
231 Tottenham Court Road, London W1P 9AE; 071-631 1546

United Nations Association of Great Britain & Northern Ireland
3 Whitehall Court, London SW1A 2EL; 071-930 2931

United Nations Information Centre
Ship House, 20 Buckingham Gate, London SW1E 6LB; 071-630 1981

Voluntary Service Overseas
317 Putney Bridge Road, London SW15 2PN; 081-780 2266